SUFFOLK PLACE-NAMES
Their Origins and Meanings

A. D. MILLS

Published by the author

ISBN 978-0-9930363-0-9

Typeset, printed and bound by
The Lavenham Press Ltd,
Lavenham, Suffolk

PREFACE

This short guide to the place-names of Suffolk, pending the full survey being undertaken by the English Place-Name Society, is born out of my delight to be living in this beautiful county and my curiosity about its intriguing names. I would like to record my thanks to the archivists at Bury and Ipswich for their help in preparing material for this book and to Alex Ford of The Lavenham Press Ltd for his design work and advice. I humbly acknowledge the work of previous authors on the subject, notably Skeat and Ekwall for their pioneering contributions, but also the other authors listed in the Select Bibliography. In particular I would like to thank all my colleagues past and present for our many useful discussions over the years. However I do of course take sole responsibility for the views finally proposed in the book, as well as for any errors or deficiencies remaining.

David Mills
Beech Tree Cottage, Monks Eleigh
Suffolk   IP7 7JE

a.d.mills@btinternet.com

July 2014

This book is dedicated to my dearest wife Solvejg
in gratitude for her patience, love and loyal support

CONTENTS

INTRODUCTION

There is a perennial fascination about the origins and meanings of place-names, those familiar but often curious labels for places, not least in a county like Suffolk that is blessed with such a splendid variety of them. The place-names of Suffolk are an important, colourful and distinctive part of its rich heritage. They are as full of interesting diversity as its beautiful scenery and landscape, and even the most familiar names will often have an unexpected origin and meaning. This book sets out to provide all those who know Suffolk, whether fortunate enough to live in the county or only passing through, with information about the origins of its place-names, their history, their underlying meaning and their significance.

The alphabetical list of Suffolk place-names includes some seven hundred names of towns, villages, hamlets and rivers, all of them found on the latest editions of the excellent 1:50000 maps published by the Ordnance Survey in the Landranger Series. The main object of this dictionary is simple – to explain the most likely meanings and origins of the names in a clear, concise, and easily accessible form, based on the evidence so far available. Most of the names have of course been listed and discussed before in various specialized studies as well as in dictionaries of a more general nationwide kind (*see* Select Bibliography for Further Reading), but exactly a century since Walter Skeat's ground-breaking *The Place-Names of Suffolk* was published, it seemed a propitious time to produce another book dedicated only to Suffolk which will at least bring things reasonably up to date with the latest research. Of course the much more detailed investigation of the county's names being undertaken by the English Place-Name Society, as part of The Survey of English Place-Names, will eventually provide richer material from an abundance of sources, deeper analysis and discussion, and a definitive account, but publication of this series of volumes is still some years away.

Each entry in the present list provides some basic information about the history and origin of the name, as far as it is known: (*a*) its modern form as it appears on map or signpost; (*b*) some representative early spellings (printed in italics) for the name, with dates, to show how the name has developed (when the name occurs in a particularly interesting early record, like an Anglo-Saxon charter or Domesday Book, this is mentioned); (*c*) the probable original meaning of the name, deduced from the evidence of early spellings so far available (both those cited here and in other more detailed studies); (*d*) the elements (i.e. words) or personal names from which the name is derived, cited in their original spelling and language (the elements are also listed in the Glossary at the end of the book); (*e*) other brief comments where appropriate on points of linguistic, geographical, or historical interest.

Suffolk place-names and their meanings
Most people will have wondered at some time or other about the original meaning of a place-name, and it is certainly the case that many of Suffolk's towns and villages have delightful, interesting and indeed curious names. Who can fail to be intrigued by names like **Bricett**, **Cattawade**, **Copdock**, **Snape** and **Shimpling**? Why **Bildeston** and **Boulge**, **Eye** and **Iken**, **Rattlesden** and **Rishangles**? How did **Knodishall**, **Nedging Tye** and **Walberswick** get their names? What on earth does **Wetheringsett** or **Kettlebaston** mean?

In fact all of these Suffolk names, like most of the names listed in this book, have original meanings that are not at all apparent from their modern forms. That is because most older place-names today are what could be termed 'linguistic fossils'. Although they originated as living units of speech – coined by our distant ancestors as descriptions of places in terms of their topography, appearance, situation, use, ownership or other association – most have become, in the course of time, mere labels, no longer possessing a clear linguistic meaning. This is not surprising when one considers that many place-names are a thousand years old or more, and are expressed in vocabulary that may have evolved differently from the equivalent words in the ordinary language, or that may now be completely extinct or obscure. It is only by tracing each name back to its earliest spellings in the records that its original meaning can be discovered and its original significance appreciated.

Of course it is true that a few Suffolk names like **Easton** and **Norton** are found in other counties, but most are quite unique (there are no other **Eykes** or **Lavenhams** or **Southwolds** or **Wetheringsetts** outside Suffolk). All these names are ancient, taking us back to the great historical records like the Domesday Book of 1086 and to the even older Anglo-Saxon charters and wills, and often to the very beginnings of settlement history for these places. Many of course have changed a great deal since they were first coined over a thousand years ago, but all reveal fascinating information about the language and dialect, as well as about the settlement, landscape, and social history, of the region.

A few names, even very old ones, have apparently changed little through the centuries and may still convey something of their original meaning. Thus old names like **Ashfield**, **Rushbrooke** and **Woodbridge** are shown by their early spellings to be virtually self-explanatory. But such instant etymologies are often a delusion. The modern form of a name can never be assumed to convey its original meaning without early spellings to confirm it, and indeed many names prove to have quite unexpected meanings in the light of the evidence of early records. We find for instance that **Crowfield** is not named from the bird (in spite of the attractive village sign recently unveiled with its three crows) but from an Old English word *crōh* meaning 'nook or corner', that **Coney Weston** has nothing to do with rabbits but is named from an Old Scandinavian word *konungr* 'king', that **Woolpit** has no connection with the local cloth trade but is named from 'a pit for trapping wolves', that **Lakenheath** is not named from a heath but derives from a dialect form of the Old English word *hȳth* 'landing-place', and that **Herringfleet** has nothing to do with fishing boats but is 'the creek or stream (Old English *flēot*) of Herela's people'!

Names then can never be taken at face value, but can only be correctly interpreted after the careful scrutiny of the earliest attested spellings in the light of the relevant linguistic, historical and geographical factors. This is best illustrated by comparing pairs of apparently identical names that prove to have quite distinct etymologies. Thus **Thurston** near Bury St Edmunds differs in origin from **Thurston** near Hawkedon, even though each is named from an early lord of the manor with an Old Scandinavian name. **Wangford** near Lakenheath and **Wangford** near Southwold contain quite different Old English words. **Acton** is not the expected 'oak-tree estate' but instead 'Āca's estate'.

For some names, of course, even early spellings (at least those at present available) do not always provide a clear unambiguous etymology, hence the good number of names for which alternative, or only tentative, explanations are suggested. In some of these, the nature of the word occurring as first element is uncertain, as in **Brockford**, **Hitcham**, and **Redgrave**. In others it cannot be determined whether the first element is a significant word or a personal name (often derived from that same word), as in **Boyton**, **Buxhall**, **Cattishall** and **Knettishall**. Indeed not all place-names can be satisfactorily explained, even in terms of alternative possibilities. A few names, like **Sapiston** and **Sotterley**, remain partly obscure, and for others, like **Kesgrave**, **Martlesham** and **Ringshall**, the suggested etymologies are uncertain and unresolved.

The sheer variety of Suffolk names is remarkable. There are many names of the so-called simplex type, that is short names that consist of only one element, such as **Brome**, **Eye**, **Eyke**, **Hoo**, **Rede**, **Snape**, **Stoven**, **Thwaite**, **Wade**, and the several examples of **Stoke**, **Stow** and **Thorpe** (most of which have later had distinguishing words added). The large majority of names however are compounds, that is they consist of two elements, the first usually qualifying the second, as in most of the names so far mentioned. Of course many of these have undergone some degree of reduction or contraction since they were first coined. They may have been considerably changed by centuries of use in speech, hence the fact that many may retain a more conservative spelling in spite of a much reduced local pronunciation: where this is unusual or differs from the expected pronunciation of a name, it is noted in the Alphabetical List for a good many names such as **Babergh**, **Hollesley**, and **Sproughton**.

The tendency for long vowels to be shortened in compound place-names, together with weakening of stress at the end of names, results in some originally distinct elements coinciding in form and pronunciation. Thus it is not always possible to be sure whether a number of place-names, such as **Farnham**, **Horham** and **Parham**, contain the Old English habitative element *hām* 'homestead' or the quite separate topographical element *hamm* 'enclosure, river-meadow'. The same factors lead to the eventual confusion in some names of Old English *stān* 'stone' with *tūn* 'farmstead' (**Chediston** is from *stān*, **Drinkstone** is from *tūn*), and of *denu* 'valley' with *dūn* 'hill' (**Hundon** is from *denu*, **Darmsden** is from *dūn*).

Some names that go back to the Old English period still contain archaic grammatical features of the pre-Conquest language. The medial -*n*- that survives in names like **Akenham**, **Blakenham**, **Coddenham**, **Dodnash**, **Lavenham** and **Tuddenham** is what remains of an old genitive (i.e. possessive) ending in Old English. In **Henham** and **Henley** the medial -*n*- represents the survival of an old dative ending of the adjective, and in **Ballingdon** the medial -*ing*- is simply a later analogical spelling of the same ending. Another name that contains part of an old grammatical ending (in this case the initial *N*-) is **Nayland**, and the spelling of **Cattawade** seems to preserve the old genitive plural ending -*a*- in *catta* 'of the cats'. How remarkable that these old grammatical inflections have survived (if in fossilized form), and are still in use (perhaps without our realizing it), in our place-names.

As in other English counties, an enormous number of old words, now lost from the language, are embedded and survive in the early place-names of Suffolk: words like **balg* 'rounded' in **Ballingdon**, *bēag* 'ring' in **Wilby**, *edisc* 'pasture' in **Cavendish**, *tōt* 'look-out place' in **Tostock**, *worth* 'enclosure' in **Ickworth**, and very many more (*see* the Glossary of Elements for further examples). The old spoken dialect of medieval Suffolk is also still reflected in the form and development of some place-names. The names **Melford, Mellis** and **Mells** (possibly also **Melton**) contain an old south-eastern dialect form *mell* of the word *mill* (from Old English *myln*), and the same dialect feature (of *e* for Old English *y*) survives in the spellings of some ten other Suffolk names (among them **Gedding, Kenton, Mendham** and **Nedging**). It is also evidenced in early spellings such as *Haverhell* 1158 for **Haverhill** and accounts for the development of Old English *hȳth* in **Lakenheath**. Names of much more recent origin, from the post-medieval period, often incorporate old dialect words (as in names like **Beck Row, Bower House Tye, Breckland, The Gull** and **Hulver Street**).

There are a few interesting instances among Suffolk place-names of a process sometimes known as 'folk etymology' or 'popular etymology'. This is a tendency for a name to be rationalized or reinterpreted once its original meaning has been obscured or lost – because words have gone out of use, or because the person commemorated in the name has been forgotten, or because of changes in pronunciation or spelling. A nice example is in the name of **St Cross South Elmham**, where a saint has been (as it were) created from a local place-name affix *Sandcroft*, the new affix then conforming neatly to the church dedications of the other South Elmham parishes. Another case is **Herringfleet**, originally *Herlingflet*: the place is situated some four miles inland but close enough to the fishing grounds off Lowestoft for the transformation of the first element to seem appropriate. Popular etymology may have played a part in the development of other place-names like **Coney Weston, Crowfield** and **Landguard**. In all these names, familiar words which are quite unhistorical but which make a kind of sense, have replaced unfamiliar or obscure words. Popular etymology also sometimes results in a process known as 'back-formation', a phenomenon that accounts for a number of Suffolk river-names, most of them created in relatively recent times (they will almost all have had earlier names, *see* below). Thus **Glem** came to be the name of the river at **Glemsford** because the village name (historically 'the ford where *glēam* or revelry takes place') came to be understood (falsely) as 'the ford on the stream called the Glem'. Other examples of river-names resulting from back-formation include the **Alde** from **Aldeburgh**, the **Box** from **Boxford**, the **Brett** from **Brettenham, Chad Brook** from **Chadacre**, the **Deben** from **Debenham**, the **Glem** (a second instance) from **Glemham**, the **Ore** from **Orford**, the **Rat** from **Rattlesden**, the **Tang** from **Tangham**, the **Lark** from **Lackford** and the **Wren** from **Wrentham** (the last two apparently inspiring the naming of other streams from birds: the **Dove** and the **Linnet**).

Of course popular etymology, or at least the rationalization and misinterpretation of old place-names based on their current spellings, is still alive and well. Indeed some of the mistaken explanations proposed are so wild and fanciful or even ludicrous as to almost deserve a study of their own. A few examples will have to suffice. In recent publications **Bricett** has been explained as 'brightly seated' because of its sunny aspect, **Darsham** is 'the place of the deer', **Gazeley** is so called because one can gaze towards Ely from the high ground here, and **Winston** is 'the place of wine'. In some cases, the false interpretation has led to what amounts to a colourful legend, as when **Woolpit** is claimed to have been named from the famous Anglo-Danish Ealdorman of East Anglia, Ulfketill Snilling, who granted this and other estates to St Edmund's abbey at Bury *c.*1000, or when **Woolverstone** is said to be the place where a Viking king Wulf sacrificed a local maiden on a monolithic stone! In the case of **Ipswich**, the myth still persists (in spite of Skeat's firm dismissal of it as long ago as 1913) that the first part of the name is shared with that of the River **Gipping**, a mistaken analysis of early spellings like *Gipeswic* which in fact would have been pronounced 'yipswich'. Hopefully the etymologies put forward in this book, however interim and conjectural they may be for some names, but based as they are on the best evidence at present available, will prove to be just as interesting as these colourful concoctions.

By far the great majority of Suffolk town and village names are of Anglo-Saxon origin, that is they result from the invasions and settlement of Germanic tribes (mainly Angles) here from the 5th century onwards. They came at first as mercenaries to the Romans but eventually as conquerors and settlers in their own right. Although the native Britons and the Romans had farmed here for centuries, and the archaeological evidence for their presence is abundant, most of their place-names seem not to have survived. Thus such majestic Romano-British place-names as *Camboritum* ('the crooked ford', probably where the Icknield Way crosses the River Lark near **Icklingham**), *Combretovium* ('at the confluence', a Roman site on the River Gipping at **Baylham**), and *Sitomagus* ('the wide field or market', a lost site somewhere near Dunwich or Aldeburgh), all mentioned in the 4th century Antonine Itinerary, disappeared from use. Just a few names of Celtic (or at least pre-English) origin survive, enough at least to reinforce the evidence (provided by Anglo-Saxon names such as Walton and Wickham, *see* below) for some sort of continuity and contact between the Romano-Britons and their English-speaking conquerors. The first part of the name **Orwell** is an ancient Celtic river-name *Arwe*, the first element of **Charsfield** may be an old Celtic river-name *Cear*, the name of the **Little Ouse** is pre-English, the name of the **Kennet** (also recurring as the first element of **Kentwell**) is Celtic, and the **Stour** may also be of Celtic origin. The river-name that gives name to **Clare** is first recorded in a Latin form and may also belong to this period. Particularly informative are the original names (*Amalburnan* and *Mearcella*) recorded for the Rivers **Box** and **Brett** (this with a crossing at **Cosford**, named from the Celtic word *cors* 'a marsh'): *Amal-* and *Mearcella* are probably of Celtic origin. Many such names, of places as well as rivers, must have been replaced or forgotten as the Angles made their settlements and described the landscape they found, perhaps sometimes taking over existing farms or working alongside native Britons, sometimes clearing more woodland or breaking in new ground for cultivation, at the same time establishing their own social and administrative systems, and (once they had been christianised in the 7th century) building churches.

Folk names and habitative names

Particularly interesting among the many names of Anglo-Saxon origin are the so-called 'folk names', in which the settlement is named from the group-name of the settlers themselves. Among these are **Barking**, **Gipping** and **Shimpling** ('the settlements of the family or followers of men called Berica, Gyppa and Scimpel'). Although most names of this type contain the personal name of the tribal leader, **Bealings** may be 'the people of the funeral pyre', perhaps then referring to a community which practised cremation in a predominantly inhumation culture (as is also possible in **Belton** and **Belstead**). In other Suffolk names (as many as thirty or so), the name of a tribe or family of settlers is combined with another element, so that **Bedingfield** is 'the open land (*feld*) of Beda's people', **Dallinghoo** is 'the hill-spur (*hōh*) of Dalla's people', and **Framlingham** 'the homestead (*hām*) of Framela's people'. At least some of these ancient names probably belong to the earlier part of the Anglo-Saxon period when tribal identities were still important.

A great many Suffolk place-names from the Anglo-Saxon period describe habitation sites, whether homesteads, farmsteads or enclosures, in terms of their ownership, topography or other association at the time the name was coined, usually at least a thousand years ago. Among these by far the most frequent final elements are Old English *hām* 'homestead' and *tūn* 'farmstead' (each of them eventually coming to mean 'manor, estate, village'). There are some eighty examples of Suffolk names formed from *hām* and over a hundred from *tūn*. Thus **Lavenham** and **Saxmundham** are 'the homesteads of men called Lāfa and Seaxmund', **Debenham** is 'the homestead on the river called *Dēope* (the deep one)', **Dalham** is 'the valley homestead', **Blundeston** and **Sproughton** are 'the farmsteads of men called Blunt and Sprow', and **Wissington** is 'the farmstead of a woman called Wīgswīth'.

However the relative chronology of these two categories of name is significant. It has been convincingly shown that in general the names in *hām* belong to the earlier part of the Anglo-Saxon period, to a time of primary settlement from the 5th to the 7th century, whereas the names in *tūn* are more likely to belong to the later part of the period, from the 8th century onwards (even though of course the settlements they describe may have been ancient, with the implication that the Anglo-Saxon name may often have replaced an earlier one). It is certainly the case that many of the names containing *hām* appear to be closely related in their distribution to the system of Roman roads and ancient trackways, to Romano-British settlements and villas, and to pagan Anglo-Saxon burial sites, all evidence suggesting that they belong to the early phases of settlement. Among the many possible examples, there are Romano-British settlement sites at **Baylham**, **Coddenham**, **Hitcham**, **Santon Downham** and **Stonham**, and Romano-British dwelling sites and villas are known at **Brettenham**, **Pakenham**, **Rougham**, **Wattisham** and **Welnetham**. Roman pottery and other items indicating occupation have been found at (among other places) **Barnham**, **Blakenham**, **Lavenham** and **Mendham**, and a Romano-British cemetery has been discovered at **Ingham**. In addition, many of the places named from *hām* are closely associated with pagan Anglo-Saxon burial sites, among them **Akenham**, **Barham**, **Barsham**, **Coddenham**, **Fakenham**, **Finningham**, **Fornham**, **Freckenham**, **Gisleham**, **Icklingham**, **Langham**, **Rendlesham** (also of course the site of the Anglo-Saxon royal hall of the *Wuffingas*), and **Wortham**.

Particularly significant in this connection are the three Suffolk names derived from the Old English compound *wīc-hām* 'homestead associated with a Romano-British settlement': **Wickhambrook**, **Wickham Market** and **Wickham Skeith**. At each of these places there is archaeological evidence for a Romano-British settlement nearby, and taken together with other Suffolk names like Bulcamp, Campsea Ashe, Walpole and Walton (*see* below), they strongly support the evidence for continuity of settlement and for the survival and continued presence of a native British population into the Anglo-Saxon period.

Other important habitative elements include Old English *burh* 'stronghold, fortified place' (as in **Blythburgh** 'the stronghold on the river Blyth'), *stede* 'settlement site' (as in **Polstead** 'the pool settlement'), *stoc* 'outlying farmstead' (as in **Stoke by Clare**), *stow* 'assembly place, holy place' (as in **Stowmarket** and **West Stow**), *wīc* 'harbour, trading centre' (in **Dunwich**, **Ipswich**, and **Walberswick**), and *worth* 'enclosed farmstead' (as in **Chelsworth** 'the enclosure of the freeman, or of a man called Ceorl'). Many of these names too, especially those from *burh*, *stow* and *stede*, may well belong to the earlier part of the Anglo-Saxon period. Indeed several of the names containing *burh* link in a significant way with the early archaeology of the county: **Aldeburgh** refers to a lost Roman site, as does the ***Burg*** at Felixstowe, and both **Burgh** (near Grundisburgh) and **Burgh Castle** (now Norfolk) refer to known Roman sites. The large Anglo-Saxon settlement at West Stow dates from the 5th century.

Topographical names and the Suffolk landscape
The place-names of Suffolk reflect every aspect of its scenery and landscape, seen through the eyes of its earlier inhabitants. The importance of rivers, streams and pools for early settlement is shown in names like **Holbrook** ('the hollow brook'), **Sudbourne** ('the southern stream'), **Semer** ('the lake pool'), and **Elmswell** ('the spring or stream where elm-trees grow'). The many places that take their names from fords (over twenty in Suffolk), like **Bramford** ('the broom ford'), **Chillesford** ('the gravel ford') and **Stratford** ('the ford on a Roman road'), show the early importance of river crossings for communications and trade. **Cattawade** on the River Stour is 'the ford or crossing place frequented by wildcats'. The several settlements (some eight in all) named from the important early settlement term Old English *ēg* 'island' (usually referring to a patch of higher dry ground in an otherwise marshy area) include **Bawdsey** ('Baldhere's island'), **Bungay** ('the island at the raised neck of land'), and of course **Eye** itself, whilst the related word *ēg-land* with similar meaning gives name to **Nayland**.

Other topographical features and aspects of the gently undulating Suffolk landscape are well represented. Hills or relatively higher ground are referred to in names containing Old English *beorg* 'hill or mound' (as in **Finborough** 'the woodpecker hill'), *dūn* 'hill, down, large area of raised ground' (as in **Brandon** 'the broom-covered hill' and ten other names), *hōh* 'hill-spur' (as in **Wixoe** 'the hill-spur of a man called Widuc'), and *hyll* 'hill' (**Haverhill** 'oats or goat hill'). Valleys or hollows are referred to in names containing Old English *denu* 'valley' (as in **Frostenden** 'the valley frequented by frogs' and **Wantisden** 'Want's valley') and *dæl* (as in **Botesdale** 'Bōtwulf's valley'). There are several settlements named from the Old English term *halh* 'nook, hollow' (as in **Blaxhall** 'Blæc's hollow' and **Spexhall** 'green woodpecker's nook').

Not surprisingly, in a county once heavily forested, many old place-names refer to woodland. The important Old English element *lēah* 'wood or woodland clearing' occurs in over twenty Suffolk names, and is usually taken to indicate woodland which the Anglo-Saxons recognized as ancient. Such name include **Cranley** ('the woodland clearing frequented by cranes'), **Hadleigh** ('the heathy woodland clearing'), and **Hinderclay** and **Eleigh** ('the woodland estates of men called Hildrīc and Illa'): in the latter the distinguishing affixes **Brent** 'burnt' and **Monks** (alluding to possession by the monks of Canterbury) first appear in the early 14th century. Other woodland terms include Old English *holt* (in **Occold** 'the oak wood'), *grāf(a)* (in **Palgrave** 'the grove where poles are got'), *hyrst* (in **Hartest** 'the wooded hill frequented by harts or stags') and *weald* 'forest' (in **Southwold** 'the southern forest').

More open stretches of land, perhaps already cleared at an earlier date, gave rise to the many settlement names (some thirty in Suffolk) containing the Old English word *feld* 'open land without trees (originally used for pasture)'. Examples include **Mickfield** ('the large tract of open land'), **Stanningfield** ('the stony open land'), **Waldingfield** ('the open land of the forest dwellers') and **Whatfield** 'the open land used for wheat'). Many of these names in *feld*, like some of the other topographical names in *ēg*, *ford* and *dūn* (*see* above), may well have been given to settlements in the early part of the Anglo-Saxon period. Many other names provide information about the agricultural economy of earlier times, for instance names like **Raydon** and **Reydon** (both 'the hill where rye is grown'), **Benacre** ('the arable land where beans are grown'), **Cornard** ('the arable used for corn'), **Hardwick** ('the livestock farm'), **Peasenhall** ('the nook where peas grow'), **Shipmeadow** ('the sheep meadow'), **Swilland** ('the swine pasture'), and **Wetherden** ('the valley where wether-sheep are kept'). It will be noted that several of these names (among others) show the very early importance of sheep-rearing and corn-growing in the county. Also of particular interest are the two names **Bulcamp** and **Campsea Ashe** which contain Old English *camp* 'a field or enclosure' (an early borrowing of Latin *campus*): these support the evidence provided by names like Wickham (*see* above) and Walton (*see* below) for continuity of settlement, and for the survival of a native British element in the population into Anglo-Saxon times.

It is clear from this small selection of names that our Anglo-Saxon ancestors made use of a vast vocabulary in a very practical and specific way to describe their various settlements and the landscape around them. The natural history of Suffolk is also well represented among its place-names. Well over thirty different species of tree and plant are evidenced, in names like **Alderton** ('the farmstead where alders grow', **Aspall** ('the aspen-tree nook'), **Copdock** ('the pollarded oak-tree') and **Kersey** ('the island/promontory where cress grows'). Some of the several names referring to wild animals and birds have already been noted, and to these can be added (among others) **Foxhall** ('the fox's earth'), **Woolpit** ('the wolf pit'), and **Yaxley** ('the cuckoo clearing'). Even insects apparently make an appearance a thousand years ago in **Braiseworth** and **Great Bricett** (probably 'the enclosure and fold infested with gadflies') and in **Knettishall** (possibly 'the nook infested with gnats'), and a fish (the trout) gives its name to **Fornham**.

Some further points of linguistic and historical interest
There is good evidence among the names of a multi-cultural society over a millennium ago. Within this predominantly Anglian area, settlements of peoples other than Angles are recognized and acknowledged. Folk of other Germanic stock are identified in **Flempton** 'the farmstead of the Flemings (natives of Flanders)', **Freston** and **Friston** 'the farmsteads of the Frisian or Frisians (from Friesland)', **Saxham** 'the homestead of the Saxons', and perhaps also in **Ingham** (possibly 'the homestead of the Inguione'). Particularly important and significant are the four names that confirm (along with the evidence of the Wickhams and the river-names of Celtic or pre-English origin) the survival and continued presence of the native British population into Anglo-Saxon times: **Brettenham** and **Walsham** are both 'the homestead of the Briton', **Walpole** is 'the pool of the Britons', and **Walton** is 'the farmstead of the Britons'.

In addition to these, most interestingly, over thirty place-names remind us that Suffolk was once under Danish rule: as part of the Danelaw, that great swathe of eastern and northern England, for several decades in the years after the Viking invasions of 865, and again later, in the early 11th century, when England became part of a large Scandinavian empire under Canute. Some names are purely Danish, others are hybrids (a mix of Danish and English, in which an Old Scandinavian word or personal name is compounded with an Old English term). Some of the older names may suggest that after the attacks ceased many of the Viking warriors settled to become farmers (no doubt perhaps also marrying Anglo-Saxon women). Solidly Scandinavian names include **Ashby** (the ash-tree farmstead'), **Barnby** ('the farmstead of the young heirs'), **Eyke** ('the place at the oak-tree'), **Lound** ('the small wood or grove'), **Risby** ('the brushwood farmstead'), **Thingoe** ('the assembly mound'), **Thwaite** ('the clearing'), **Thorpe** ('the secondary settlement'), and of course **Lowestoft** ('Hlothvér's homestead'). Many of the hybrid names are from Old English *tūn* with an Old Scandinavian personal name, thus perhaps describing places taken over by, or granted to, Vikings or their descendants during the periods of Danish rule.

They include **Bildeston**, **Drinkstone**, **Kettlebaston** and **Thrandeston** ('the farmsteads of men called Bildr, Drengr, Ketilbiorn and Thrandr'. Three of the names contain personal names that actually recall the Viking roots of their bearers and the expeditions of their ancestors: **Somerleyton** and **Somerton** are 'the farmsteads of Sumarlithi (the summer traveller)', and **Westleton** is 'the farmstead of Westlithi (the traveller to the west)'. Other hybrid names include the two examples of **Carlton** ('the estate of the freemen'), **Coney Weston** ('the king's estate'), **Ilketshall** ('*Ylfketill's land-unit'), **Kirkley** and **Kirton** ('the church clearing and estate'), and **Minsmere** ('the river-mouth pool'). Perhaps most unusual is the significant affix (from the Old Scandinavian word *skeith* 'race-course for horses') added to the existing Old English name in **Wickham Skeith**.

By way of contrast, the Norman-French influence on Suffolk place-names is only slight. Only very few names are French in origin, in spite of the far-reaching effects of the Norman conquest on the English language in general. It is clear that by 1066, most major settlements and landscape features already had established names, and the new Norman aristocracy only rarely gave French names to their estates. However **Boulge** (?'the uncultivated heathland') is possibly a Norman-French name, as are **Capel St Andrew** and **St Mary** ('the places with a chapel'): the word *capel* is a northern Old French form of the word *chapel*. The influence of this French-speaking aristocracy is also revealed in the way the names of powerful feudal families were affixed to the names of the manors they possessed. These manorial additions result in a number of hybrid 'double-barrelled' names, some of them still colourful and even a touch exotic: **Bradfield St Clare**, **Carlton Colville**, **Easton Bavents**, **Stowlangtoft**, and **Thorpe Morieux** all have affixes from the Norman-French family-names (derived from place-names in France) of their manorial lords in medieval times. Anglo-Norman lords are also commemorated in **Ashbocking** and **Stonham Aspal** (the families came from Bocking in Essex and Aspall in Suffolk). In the name **Walsham le Willows**, the survival of the French definitive article is also a sign of this Norman-French influence.

Of course not all names on the modern map are as old as those (mostly names of parishes, towns and villages) so far mentioned. Many names of smaller settlements, villages, hamlets, farmsteads and even topographical features probably originate in the Middle English period, that is from the 12th to 15th century inclusive. Names such as **Botesdale**, **Boxford**, **Leavenheath**, **Pettistree** and **Wentford** probably belong here. Others may turn out to go back to the medieval period (once earlier recorded spellings are available), or they may be of more recent origin: these might include some of the many hamlet-names in *-Green*, *-Street* and *-Tye* (such as **Coldfair Green**, **Fingal Street** and **Bower House Tye**) and names such as **Beck Row** and **Buss Creek**. Some names certainly originate in much more recent times. The commemorative name **Bunker's Hill** dates from the 18th century, as does the whimsical **Little London**. Other transferred names like **California**, **Dublin** and **Gibraltar** (surprising to find these in Suffolk!) are of 19th century or later origin.

The place-names of Suffolk reflect many different aspects of its social and economic history. **Covehithe**, **Lakenheath** and **Wherstead** refer to early landing-places, whilst **Dunwich**, **Ipswich** and **Walberswick** also allude to harbours and trading settlements. Other references to economic activity include the several places named from mills and markets such as **Melford** and **Stowmarket**. Some names (**Mutford**, **Thingoe**, **Shadingfield**) refer to the ancient meeting-places or boundaries of medieval Hundreds, and **Tostock** is named from an early look-out place. Three names (**Barnham**, **Freckenham** and **Thurlow**) may refer to warriors. Others illustrate the structure of medieval society, in that various social ranks are represented among the early names: kings and princes (**Coney Weston**, **Kingston**, **Athelington**), noblemen (**Earl Soham**, **Earl Stonham**), youths and young heirs (**Barnby**, **Chilton**), freemen or peasants (**Bruisyard**, **Carlton**, **Chelsworth**), and servants (**Boyton**).

Many individuals are recalled, and in a sense commemorated, in Suffolk place-names. In the many place-names from the Anglo-Saxon period, some of the men who bore Old English names, like the Lāfa who gave name to **Lavenham** or the Tud(d)a who gave name to **Tuddenham**, may have been among the early Anglian settlers who colonized Suffolk from the 5th century onwards, but many were no doubt thegns who had been granted their estates by kings or bishops at a somewhat later date, probably between the 7th and the 10th century, and others may have been farmers or relatively humble peasants. Nothing more is known about most of these individuals other than what the names tell us, but a few have been identified with known historical figures, such as the 7th century bishop who may be commemorated in **Chediston** or the 8th century moneyer who probably gave his name to **Euston**. The great majority of landowners who gave their names to estates in the Anglo-Saxon period were men, but interestingly and significantly, four estates (**Alpheton**, **Alton**, **Dennington** and **Wissington**) are named from women, some of whom may have been the widows or daughters of thegns who had earlier owned the estates. Of particular note is the fact that the woman who gave her name to Alpheton can be identified from other historical sources.

Some Suffolk place-names provide fascinating glimpses into the beliefs, pastimes and recreations of early times. **Elveden** may allude to some popular superstition. Three names seem to confirm that our distant ancestors knew how to have a good time. **Glemham** and **Glemsford** from the Old English word *glēam* indicate that these places were 'the homestead and the ford noted for their revelry and games', and **Playford** means 'the ford where play or sport takes place' – fords (and bridges) seem to have been particularly popular gathering places in medieval times. From a somewhat later date, May festivities are referred to in the two examples of **Maypole Green**. Huntsmen are referred to in the names **Hunston** and **Huntingfield**, and there may also be some evocation of hunting in the name **Hartest** ('the wooded hill frequented by harts or stags'). And then there is **Wickham Skeith** – how remarkable, and intriguing, that there was horse-racing in Suffolk long before Newmarket evolved into the pre-eminent home of the sport (although races are recorded here from the early 17th century)!

This Introduction has only touched upon a few of the points of interest arising from a study of the place-names of Suffolk. Naturally much more information can be gleaned from the individual entries in the Alphabetical List of Names, from the Glossary of Elements that follows, and from the various studies listed in the Select Bibliography at the end of the book.

ALPHABETICAL LIST OF
SUFFOLK PLACE-NAMES

Acton *Acantun* 1000-2 (in an 11th century copy of an Anglo-Saxon will), *Achetuna* 1086 (Domesday Book). 'The farmstead or estate of a man called Āca', from an Old English personal name (genitive case -*an*) and *tūn*. The fairly common name Acton usually means 'the farmstead or estate by the oak-tree(s)' or 'the specialized farm where oak timber is worked', from Old English *āc* 'oak' and *tūn*, so the Suffolk Acton is rather unique.

Akenham *Acheham, Ac(h)reham* 1086 (Domesday Book), *Akenham* 1254. 'The homestead of a man called Āca', from an Old English personal name (genitive case -*an*) and Old English *hām*. The local pronunciation is 'ayken'm'.

Alde, River Recorded as *Ald* 1735, *Ald(e)* 1764, *see* Aldeburgh.

Aldeburgh *Aldeburc* 1086 (Domesday Book), *Aldeburga* 1198. 'The old or disused stronghold', from Old English *(e)ald* and *burh* (dative case *byrig*). The name refers to a pre-English fortification (a Roman site here lies under the sea). The river name **Alde** is a so-called back-formation from the place-name. The local pronunciation is 'ol-bruh' or 'awl-bruh'.

Alderton *Alretuna* 1086 (Domesday Book), *Alderton* 1254. 'The farmstead or estate where alders grow', from Old English *alor* and *tūn*. The local pronunciation is 'awlder-t'n'.

Aldham *Ealdham, Aldeham* 1086 (Domesday Book). 'The old homestead', or 'the homestead of a man called (E)alda', from Old English *hām* and either *(e)ald* 'old' or an Old English personal name. The local pronunciation is 'awld'm'. Aldham in Essex is identical in origin and meaning.

Aldringham *Alrincham* 1086 (Domesday Book), *Alringeham* 1199, *Aldringham* 1275. 'The homestead of the family or followers of a man called Aldhere', from an Old English personal name with *-inga-* (genitive case of *-ingas* 'people of') and *hām*. The local pronunciation is 'awldring'm'.

All Saints South Elmham, *see* Elmham.

Alnesbourn Priory (near Nacton) Marked on the Ordnance Survey map of 1805, named from *Aluesbrunna* [*sic*, for *Alnes-*] 1086 (Domesday Book), *Alnesburn* 1250, 'the stream of a man called Ælfwine', from Old English *burna* and an Old English personal name. There was a small Augustinian priory here.

Alpheton *Alfledetun* 1186-91, *Alflede(s)ton* 1204, *Alfeton* 1254. 'The farmstead or estate of a woman called Ælfflǣd', from an Old English personal name and *tūn*. This is one of the four Suffolk places named from an Anglo-Saxon female landowner (in this case possibly to be associated with a known historical figure, the lady called *Elflet* or *Alflet* mentioned in Domesday Book as holding estates in this area in 1066). The local pronunciation is 'al-fee-t'n' (with the stress on the second syllable).

Alton Water (near Holbrook) Named from Alton Hall, marked thus on Hodkinson's map of 1783. The name Alton is *Alsildeston* [*sic* for *Alfildeston*, with the common scribal confusion of *s* and *f*] in 1086 (Domesday Book), 'the farmstead or estate of a woman called Ælfhild', from an Old English personal name and *tūn*. This is one of the four Suffolk places named from an Anglo-Saxon female landowner.

Ampton *Hametuna* 1086 (Domesday Book), *Ameton* 1196. 'The farmstead or estate of man called *Amma', from Old English *tūn* and an Old English personal name.

Ashbocking *Assa, Essa, Hassa* 1086 (Domesday Book), *Assh* 1296, *Bokkynge Assh* 1411. Originally '(the place at) the ash-tree(s)', from Old English *æsc*, later with manorial affix from the *de Bocking* family, here in the 14th century. The family took their name from Bocking in Essex. Ash-trees still flourish here.

Ashby (near Lound) *Aschebi* 1198, *Askeby* 1254. 'The farmstead or estate where ash-trees grow', from Old Scandinavian *askr* (alternating with Old English *æsc*) and Old Scandinavian *bý*.

Ashfield cum Thorpe *Assefelda* 1086 (Domesday Book), *Esfeld* 1198. 'The open land where ash-trees grow', from Old English *æsc* (genitive case plural *æsca*) and *feld*. **Thorpe** (marked as *Thorp* on Hodskinson's map of 1783) is *Torp* 1086 (Domesday Book), *Thorpe* 1327, from Old Scandinavian *thorp* 'secondary settlement, outlying dependent farmstead or hamlet', the preposition *cum* being Latin for 'with'.

Ashfield, Great *Eascefelda* 1086 (Domesday Book), *Aysefeld Magna* 1291. Identical in origin and meaning with the previous name. The early affix is Latin *magna* 'great' (to distinguish it from Badwell Ash which was sometimes *Little Ashfield*). Ash-trees still flourish here.

Ashfield Green (one near Stradbroke, and another near Wickhambrook) Both marked thus on Hodskinson's map of 1783 and on the Ordnance Survey map of 1837, no doubt identical in origin with the previous names, with *green* 'village green, hamlet'.

Ash Street (near Semer) Marked thus on Hodskinson's map of 1783 and on the Ordnance Survey map of 1837, 'hamlet where ash-trees grow', from *ash* and *street*.

Aspall (near Debenham) *Aspala, Espala, Aspalle* 1086 (Domesday Book), *Aspehale* 1254. 'The nook of land where aspen-trees grow', from Old English *æspe* and *halh*. The local pronunciation is 'asspl'.

Assington *Asetona* 1086 (Domesday Book), *Assintona* 1175. 'The farmstead or estate belonging to, or associated with, a man called *Assa', from an Old English personal name (genitive case *-an*), or with medial connective *-ing-* ('called after'), and *tūn*.

Assington Green (near Stansfield) Marked as *Aston End Green* on Hodskinson's map of 1783 and on the Ordnance Survey map of 1837, perhaps 'the eastern farmstead or estate', from Old English *ēast* and *tūn*, later with *end* 'district of a parish, hamlet' and *green*. The current spelling may have been influenced by the previous name.

Athelington *Elyngtone* c.946 (in a 13th century copy of an Anglo-Saxon will), *Alinggeton* 1219, *Athelinton* 1234. 'The farmstead or estate of the prince or princes', from Old English *ætheling* (genitive plural *æthelinga*) and *tūn*. The local pronunciation is 'athling-t'n' or (sometimes) 'aling-t'n'.

Attleton Green (near Wickhambrook)   Marked as *Attilton Green* on Hodskinson's map of 1783, origin uncertain without earlier spellings.

Babergh (district, earlier the name of a medieval Hundred)   *Babenberga*, *Baberga* 1086 (Domesday Book), *Babberge* 1327. 'The mound or hill of a man called Babba', from an Old English personal name (genitive case -*an*) and *beorg*. The name also still survives in local names like Babergh Heath (where the Hundred meetings were formerly held), Babergh Hall and Babergh Place (all marked thus on the Ordnance Survey map of 1805) near Great Waldingfield. The local pronunciation is 'Bayber'.

Bacton   *Bachetuna* 1086 (Domesday Book), *Baketon* 1198. 'The farmstead or estate of a man called Bacca', from Old English *tūn* and an Old English personal name. Bacton in Norfolk is identical in origin and meaning.

Badingham   *Badincham* 1086 (Domesday Book), *Bedingham* 1203, *Badingham* 1254. Probably 'the homestead or village of the family or followers of a man called *Bēada*, from an Old English personal name with -*inga*- (genitive case of -*ingas* 'people of') and *hām*.

Badley (Hall & Hill) (near Combs)   *Badelea* 1086 (Domesday Book), *Baddelea* 1200. 'The woodland clearing of a man called Badda', from Old English *lēah* and an Old English personal name.

Badmondisfield Hall (near Wickhambrook)   Marked thus on the Ordnance Survey map of 1836 and as *Badmondesfield Hall* on Hodskinson's map of 1783, named from *Bademundesfelda* 1086 (Domesday Book), *Badmundesfeld* 1270, 'the open land of a man called Beadumund', from Old English *feld* and an Old English personal name.

Badwell Ash   *Badewell* 1254, *Badewelle Asfelde* 13th century. 'The spring or stream of a man called Bada', from an Old English personal name and *wella*, later with an affix from Great Ashfield (*see* above) which was eventually shortened to *Ash*.

Ballingdon (in Sudbury)   *Belindune* 1086 (Domesday Book), *Balidon* 1236. Possibly 'the rounded down or low hill', from Old English **balg* (dative case **balgan*) and Old English *dūn*.

Bardwell *Berdeuuella, Beordewella* 1086 (Domesday Book), *Berdewelle* 1190. Probably 'the spring or stream of a man called *Bearda', from an Old English personal name and *wella*.

Barham *Bercheham* 1042-66 (in a 12th century copy of an Anglo-Saxon charter), *Bercham* 1086 (Domesday Book), *Bergham* 1252. 'The homestead or village on a hill', from Old English *beorg* and *hām*. Barham in Cambridgeshire is identical in origin and meaning.

Barking *Berchinges* 1042-66 (in a 12th century copy of an Anglo-Saxon charter), *Berchingas* 1086 (Domesday Book). '(The settlement of) the family or followers of a man called *Berica', from an Old English personal name and *-ingas*. **Barking Tye** (marked thus on Hodskinson's map of 1783) contains dialect *tye* (from Old English *tēag*) 'a large common pasture'. Barking in Greater London is identical in origin and meaning.

Barnardiston *Bernardeston* 1194, 1242. 'The farmstead or estate of a man called Beornheard', from Old English *tūn* and an Old English personal name (or its Continental Germanic counterpart *Bernard*).

Barnby *Barnebei, Barneby* 1086 (Domesday Book), *Barneby* 1254. Probably 'the farmstead of the children, i.e. one held jointly by a number of heirs', from Old Scandinavian *barn* (genitive case plural *barna*) and *bý*. Alternatively, for this and other identical names in Nottinghamshire and Yorkshire, the first element may be the Old Scandinavian personal name *Barni* or *Bjarni*.

Barnham *Byornham* 975-1016 (Anglo-Saxon will), *Bernham* 1086 (Domesday Book). 'The warrior homestead', or 'the homestead of a man called Beorn', from Old English *hām* with either Old English *beorn* or an Old English personal name.

Barningham *Bernincham* 1086 (Domesday Book), *Beorningeham* c.1095. 'The homestead or village of the family or followers of a man called Beorn', from an Old English personal name with *-inga-* (genitive case of *-ingas* 'people of') and *hām*.

Barrow *Baro* 1086 (Domesday Book), *Barue* 1201. '(The place at) the wood or grove', from Old English *bearu* (in a dative form *bearwe*).

Barsham *Barsham, Bersham* 1086 (Domesday Book), *Barsham* 1196. 'The homestead or village of a man called Bār', from an Old English personal name and *hām*. Barsham in Norfolk is identical in origin and meaning.

Barton, Great *Bertuna* 945 (in a 13th century copy of an Anglo-Saxon charter), *Bertun c*.946 (in a 13th copy of an Anglo-Saxon will), *Bertuna* 1086 (Domesday Book), *Magna Bertone* 1254. 'The barley farm, the outlying grange where corn is stored', from Old English *bere-tūn* or *bær-tūn*. The early affix is Latin *magna* 'great'.

Barton Mills *Bertona, Bertunna* 1086 (Domesday Book), *Parva Bertone* 1254, *Little Barton* 1783. Identical in origin with the previous name, the distinguishing early affix being Latin *parva* 'little'. The later affix refers to watermills on the River Lark (there is still one mill here).

Battisford *Beteforda, Betesfort* 1086 (Domesday Book), *Batesford* 1191. 'The ford of a man called *Bætti*', from an Old English personal name (genitive case *-es*) and *ford*. The ford was at a crossing of a small tributary of the River Gipping. **Battisford Tye** (marked thus on Hodskinson's map of 1783) contains dialect *tye* (from Old English *tēag*) 'a large common pasture'.

Battlesea Green (near Stradbroke) Marked as *Battlesey Green* on Hodskinson's map of 1783 and as *Buttlesea Green* on the Ordnance Survey map of 1837, origin uncertain without earlier spellings.

Bawdsey *Baldeseia, Baldereseia* 1086 (Domesday Book), *Baudeseye* 1254. 'The island (of dry or higher ground in marsh) of a man called Baldhere', from Old English *ēg* and an Old English personal name.

Baxter's Green (near Ousden) Marked *Baxters Green* on Hodskinson's map of 1783, probably from the surname *Baxter* (Middle English *bakestre* 'a (female) baker') with *green* 'village green, hamlet'.

Baylham *Beleham* 1086 (Domesday Book), *Beylham* 1228. Probably 'the homestead, or the enclosure, at the river-bend', from Old English **begel* and either *hām* or *hamm*. There are marked bends in the River Gipping here. There was an important Roman settlement site (including two forts) at Baylham House, recorded as *Combretovium* 'at the confluence' in the 4th century Antonine Itinerary.

Beacon Hill (near Kesgrave) Marked thus on the Ordnance Survey map of 1805, referring to a hill where a beacon-fire was once made for signalling purposes.

Bealings, Great & Little *Belinges, parua Belinges* 1086 (Domesday Book), *Magna Belinges* 1228, *Parva Belinges* 13th century. Etymology uncertain. Possibly '(the settlement of) the dwellers on the patch of dry ground in marsh, or by the funeral pyre', from Old English **bel* or *bēl* and *-ingas*. Alternatively '(the settlement of) the family or followers of a man called Beola', from *-ingas* with an Old English personal name. The early affixes are Latin *magna* 'great' and *parva* 'little'.

Beccles *Becles* 1086 (Domesday Book), *Beclis* 1157. Probably 'the pasture by the stream', from Old English *bece* and *lǣs*. Beccles is on the River Waveney. Alternatively perhaps 'the little court', from Celtic **bacc* and **līss*.

Beck, The (a tributary of the River Waveney) From Middle English *beck* as in the next name.

Beck Row Marked thus on Hodskinson's map of 1783 and on the Ordnance Survey map of 1836, from Middle English *beck* (Old Scandinavian *bekkr*) 'small stream, brook' and *rowe* 'row of houses, hamlet'.

Bedfield *Berdefelda* [*sic*] 1086 (Domesday Book), *Bedefeld* 12th century. 'The open land of a man called Bēda or Bēada', from Old English *feld* and an Old English personal name. The Domesday spelling is erratic. Bedfield lies only 3 miles SE of Bedingfield, so the two places may well be named from the same man.

Bedingfield *Bedingefelda, Badingafelda* 1086 (Domesday Book), *Bedingefeld* 1193. 'The open land of the family or followers of a man called Bēda or Bēada', from an Old English personal name (*see* Bedfield) with *-inga-* (genitive case of *-ingas* 'people of') and *feld*.

Bell's Cross (near Henley) Marked as *Bells Cross* on Hodskinson's map of 1783 and on the Ordnance Survey map of 1837, probably from the surname *Bell* with *cross* in the sense of 'cross-roads'.

Belstead *Belesteda* 1086 (Domesday Book), *Belstede* 1198. 'The place at the patch of dry ground in marsh', or 'the place of the funeral pyre', from Old English **bel* or *bēl* and *stede*, *see* next name.

Belton (historically in Suffolk, transferred to Norfolk in the boundary change of 1974) *Beletuna* 1086 (Domesday Book), *Beleton* 1198. Possibly 'the farmstead or estate where there is a funeral pyre', from Old English *bēl* and *tūn*. Alternatively 'the farmstead or estate on a patch of dry ground in marsh' if the first element is rather Old English **bel*. Belton in Lincolnshire is identical in origin and meaning.

Benacre *Benagra* 1086 (Domesday Book), *Beanacer c.*1095. 'The cultivated plot where beans are grown', from Old English *bēan* and *æcer*. The local pronunciation is 'benna-k'r'.

Benhall Green *Benehala, Benenhala* 1086 (Domesday Book), *Benhale* 1254, *Benhall Green* 1783. 'The nook of land where beans are grown', from Old English *bēanen* and *halh*, with the later addition of *green* 'village green, hamlet'.

Benningham Hall (in Occold) *Benigham* 1243, *Beningham* 1303. 'The homestead or village of the family or followers of a man called Beonna', from an Old English personal name with *-inga-* (genitive case of *-ingas* 'people of') and *hām*.

Bentley *Benetleia* 1086 (Domesday Book), *Benteleye* 1327. 'The woodland clearing where bent-grass grows', from Old English *beonet* and *lēah*. Bentley in Essex is identical in origin and meaning.

Bergholt, East *Bercolt* 1086 (Domesday Book), *Bergholt* 1228, *Estbergholt* 1394. 'The wood on or by a hill', from Old English *beorg* and *holt*. The affix *East* distinguishes it from West Bergholt which is in Essex. The local pronunciation is 'bur-g'lt'.

Beyton *Begatona* 1086 (Domesday Book), *Beketon* 1208. 'The farmstead or estate of a woman called Bēage or of a man called Bǣga', from Old English *tūn* and an Old English personal name. Beighton in Norfolk is identical in origin and meaning.

Bildeston *Bilestuna* 1086 (Domesday Book), *Bildestone* 1166. 'The farmstead or estate of a man called Bildr', from Old English *tūn* and an Old Scandinavian personal name. The local pronunciation is 'bildus-t'n'. Bilstone in Leicestershire is probably identical in origin and meaning.

Bixley Farm & Heath (in Foxhall) Marked as *Bixley Manor Farm* on the Ordnance Survey map of 1805, named from *Bischelea* 1086 (Domesday Book), *Biskle* 13th century. Probably 'the bush-covered woodland clearing', from Old English *lēah* and an Old English **bysce* (influenced by Old Scandinavian **byski*) 'bushy copse, scrubland'.

Black Bourn, The (a tributary of Little Ouse River) Apparently the stream that gave name to the medieval Hundred of Blackbourn, recorded as *Blacbruna*, *Blacbrune* in 1086 (Domesday Book), 'the black stream' (alluding to muddy or dark-coloured water), from Old English *blæc* and *burna* (influenced by Old Scandinavian *brunnr*).

Blackheath (near Wenhaston) Marked *Black Heath* on Hodskinson's map of 1783 and on the Ordnance Survey map of 1837, perhaps an older name like the Blackheath in south London, 'the dark-coloured heathland', from *black* (Old English *blæc*) and *heath* (Old English *hæth*).

Blackthorpe (near Rougham) Marked thus on the Ordnance Survey map of 1837, perhaps an old name from Old Scandinavian *thorp* 'secondary settlement, outlying farmstead or hamlet'.

Blakenham, Great & Little *Blacheham*, *Blacham* 1086 (Domesday Book), *Blakenham Parva* 1254, *Blakenham Magna* 1291. Probably 'the homestead of a man called Blaca', from an Old English personal name (genitive case *-an*) and Old English *hām*. The early affixes are Latin *magna* 'great' and *parva* 'little. The local pronunciation is 'blayk'n'm'.

Blaxhall *Blaccheshala* 1086 (Domesday Book), *Blakeshal* 1270. 'The nook of land or hollow belonging to a man called Blæc', from Old English *halh* and an Old English personal name.

Blundeston *Blundeston* 1203, *Blunteston* 1205. 'The farmstead or estate of a man called *Blunt*', from Old English *tūn* and an Old English personal name. The local pronunciation is 'blunder-st'n'.

Blyford *Blitleford* [*sic*, for *Blitheford*] *c*.1060 (in a 13th century copy of an Anglo-Saxon will), *Blideforda* 1086 (Domesday Book). 'The ford over the River Blyth', from the river-name ('the gentle or pleasant one', from Old English *blīthe*) and Old English *ford*.

Blyth, River Recorded as *Blith* 1586, *see* Blyford and Blythburgh.

Blythburgh *Blideburh*, *Blideburc* 1086 (Domesday Book), *Bliburgh* 1235. 'The stronghold on the River Blyth', from the river-name (*see* Blyford) and Old English *burh*. The local pronunciation is 'blithe-bruh' or (older) 'blie-bruh'.

Bosmere Hall (near Needham Market) Named from the lake by the River Gipping called Bosmere, this itself giving name to a medieval hundred recorded as *Bosemera*, *Bosemara* 1086 (Domesday Book), *Bosemere* 1205. 'The pool of a man called Bōsa', from an Old English personal name and *mere*.

Botesdale *Botholuesdal* 1275, *Botulfesdale* 1313. 'The valley of a man called Bōtwulf', from Old English *dæl* and an Old English personal name. The local pronunciation is 'bottiz-dale'.

Boulge *Bulges* 1086 (Domesday Book), *Bulge*, *Bulges* 1254. Possibly Old French *bouge* 'uncultivated land covered with heather'. The local pronunciation is 'boolj'.

Bower House Tye (near Boxford) Marked thus on the Ordnance Survey map of 1805, named from *Boxford Bower House* on the same map, from Middle English *bower* (Old English *būr*) 'a dwelling, a bower or arbour', with later addition of dialect *tye* (from Old English *tēag*) 'a large common pasture'.

Box, River (a tributary of the River Stour) Recorded as *Boxford River* 1805, *see* Boxford. An earlier name for this river is *Amalburnan* 1000-2 (in an 11th century copy of an Anglo-Saxon will), mentioned thus in a description of the Anglo-Saxon bounds of Polstead and Withermarsh, from Old English *burna* 'stream' with an uncertain first element, possibly a Celtic word **amal* 'edge, boundary'.

Boxford *Boxford* 12th century, 1254. 'The ford where box-trees grow', from Old English *box* and *ford*. The river-name **Box** is a so-called back-formation from the place-name.

Boxted *Boesteda* [*sic*, for *Bocsteda*] 1086 (Domesday Book), *Bocstede* 1154, *Boxsted* 1196. 'The place where beech-trees or box-trees grow', from Old English *bōc* or *box* and *stede*.

Boyton (near Capel St Andrew) *Boituna* 1086 (Domesday Book), *Boiton* 1196. Possibly 'the farmstead or estate of a man called Boia', from Old English *tūn* with an Old English personal name. Alternatively 'the farmstead or estate granted to a young man or servant', from the Old English word **boia* 'a boy or youth, a servant'. Another example of the same name, **Boyton End** near Stoke by Clare, and other places called Boyton in this county and in Cornwall, Essex and Wiltshire are similarly ambiguous in origin and meaning.

Bradfield Combust, Bradfield St Clare & Bradfield St George *Bradefelda* 1086 (Domesday Book), *Bradefelde Sancti Georgii* c.1186-91, *Bradefeud Sencler* 1254, *Brundbradefeld* 1321-2. 'The broad stretch of open land', from Old English *brād* and *feld*. The distinguishing affixes are from Middle English *brend* and *combust* (Latin *combusta*) 'burnt, destroyed by fire' (in allusion no doubt to some dreadful early conflagration in the village, *compare* Brent Eleigh), from early possession by the *Seyncler* family (here in 1253, from Saint Claire-sur-Elle, Manche), and from the dedication of the church to St George. Places called Bradfield in Essex and Norfolk are identical in origin and meaning.

Bradley, Great & Little *Bradeleia* 1086 (Domesday Book), *Bradeleya Magna*, *Bradeleya Parva* 1254. 'The broad woodland clearing', from Old English *brād* and *lēah*. The early distinguishing affixes are Latin *magna* 'great' and *parva* 'little'.

Bradwell (historically in Suffolk, transferred to Norfolk in the boundary change of 1974) *Bradwell* c.1210, *Bradewell* 1211. '(The place at) the broad spring or stream', from Old English *brād* and *wella*. Bradwell-on-Sea in Essex is identical in origin and meaning.

Braiseworth *Briseworde* 1086 (Domesday Book), *Briseworth* 1254. 'The enclosure infested with gadflies, or belonging to a man called *Brīosa', from Old English *worth* with either Old English *brīosa* or an Old English personal name (from the same word).

Bramfield *Brunfelda* [sic] (Domesday Book), *Bramfeld* 1166. 'The open land where broom grows', from Old English *brōm* and *feld*. One of the seven Suffolk places named from this plant: for its many uses in medieval times, *see* Brome.

31

Bramford *Bromford* 1035-44 (in a 13th century copy of an Anglo-Saxon will), *Branfort* 1086 (Domesday Book). 'The ford where broom grows', from Old English *brōm* and *ford*. There is a crossing of the River Gipping here. The local pronunciation is 'brarmf'd'.

Brampton *Bramtuna, Brantuna* 1086 (Domesday Book), *Brampton* 1242. 'The farmstead or estate where broom grows', from Old English *brōm* and *tūn*.

Brandeston *Brantestona* 1086 (Domesday Book), *Branteston* 1195. 'The farmstead or estate of a man called *Brant', from Old English *tūn* and an Old English personal name. Brandiston in Norfolk is identical in origin and meaning.

Brandon *Bromdun* 10th century, *Brandune* 1042-66 (in a 12th century copy of an Anglo-Saxon charter), *Brandona* 1086 (Domesday Book). 'The hill where broom grows', from Old English *brōm* and *dūn*. Brandon Parva in Norfolk is identical in origin and meaning.

Brantham *Brantham* 1086 (Domesday Book), *Braham* 1198. Possibly 'the homestead or enclosure of a man called *Branta', from an Old English personal name with either *hām* or *hamm*. Alternatively, the first element may be the Old English adjective *brant* 'steep' (referring to the slope up to the church from the River Stour).

Breckland (region of undulating sandy heathland in north west Suffolk) Referred to as *The Breck District* in 1866, and as *Breckland* in 1894, from dialect *breck* (Old English *brēc, brǣc*) 'land broken up for cultivation' with *land* in the sense 'district'.

Bredfield *Bredefelda, Bradefelda* 1086 (Domesday Book), *Bredefeld* 1286. 'The broad stretch of open land', from Old English *brǣdu* and *feld*.

Brent Eleigh, *see* Eleigh.

Brett, River Recorded as *Breton* 1577, *the Bretton* 1618, *Breton or Bret* 1735, *see* Brettenham. A much older (indeed the original) name of this river (from its alternative source north of Lavenham, hence the name *Lavenham Brook* sometimes now found for its main arm) right through to its confluence with the River Stour at Higham, is recorded in two sources from the Anglo-Saxon period.

It is referred to as *mearcella* in 962 (in an Anglo-Saxon charter describing the bounds of Chelsworth at that date), and as *mercyl(e)* in 1000-2 (in an 11th century copy of an Anglo-Saxon will to which is appended a description of the bounds of Polstead and Withermarsh). The meaning of this ancient river-name *mearcella* is uncertain, but a recent suggestion that it is of Celtic origin with a sense 'the little horse, the filly' is convincing.

Brettenham *Bret(t)ham*, *Bretenhama* 1086 (Domesday Book), *Brethenham* *c*.1095, *Bretenham* 1275. 'The homestead of a man called *Bretta ('the Briton')', from Old English *hām* and an Old English personal name (genitive case *-an*). This is an interesting name since, like Walpole, Walsham and Walton, it suggests some survival of a native British element in the population into Anglo-Saxon times. The east boundary of the parish follows the line of a Roman road. The name of the River **Brett**, one arm of which rises near here, is a so-called back-formation from the place-name. Brettenham in Norfolk is identical in origin and meaning.

Bricett, Great *Brieseta* 1086 (Domesday Book), *Brisete* 1198, *Magna Brisete* 1235. Probably 'the fold(s) or stable(s) infested with gadflies', from Old English *brīosa* and *(ge)set* (plural *(ge)setu*). The affix *great* (Latin *magna*) distinguishes it from Little Bricett, recorded as *Parva Briset* 1212 (Latin *parva* 'little').

Brightwell *Brithwelle* *c*.1042-66 (in a 12th century copy of an Anglo-Saxon charter), *Brithtewella* 1086 (Domesday Book). 'The bright or clear spring or stream', from Old English *beorht* and *wella*. A tributary of the River Deben called Mill River flows through here. Brightwell in Oxfordshire is identical in origin and meaning.

Broad Green (near Earl Stonham) Marked thus on Hodskinson's map of 1783 and on the Ordnance Survey map of 1837, 'the large village green or hamlet', perhaps contrasting with nearby Forward Green.

Brockford Street *Brocaforde*, *Brokeforde* 11th century (Anglo-Saxon charters), *Brocfort* 1086 (Domesday Book). 'The ford over the brook, or one frequented by badgers', from Old English *ford* with either *brōc* or *brocc* (genitive case plural *brocca*). There is a crossing of a small unnamed stream here.

Brockley (Green) (near Hartest) *Brocle*, *Broclega* 1086 (Domesday Book), *Brocleye* 1254. 'The woodland clearing by a brook, or one frequented by badgers', from Old English *lēah* with either *brōc* or *brocc*. **Brockley Green** near Kedington is no doubt identical in origin and meaning.

Brome (Street) *Brom, Brum* 1086 (Domesday Book), *Brome* 1197. 'The place where broom grows', from Old English *brōm*. The broom plant had a wide variety of uses in medieval times, not just for making brooms and baskets but also as a thatching material, as a source for dye, and even in medicine, hence perhaps the seven Suffolk place-names incorporating this word. *Street* has the sense 'hamlet'.

Bromeswell *Bromeswella, Brumeswella* 1086 (Domesday Book), *Bromeswell* 1254. Possibly 'the rising ground where broom grows', from Old English *brōm* and **swelle*. Alternatively perhaps 'the spring or stream at the place where broom grows', from Old English *brōm* (genitive case -*es*) and *wella*. The local pronunciation is 'brooms-w'l'.

Browston Green (near Belton, now Norfolk) *Brockestuna* 1086 (Domesday Book), *Broxton* 1232, *Brockeston* 1270. 'The farmstead or estate of a man called Brocc', from an Old English personal name (from the word *brocc* 'badger') and Old English *tūn*.

Bruisyard *Buresiart* 1086 (Domesday Book), *Buresgerd* 1204. 'The peasant's enclosure', from Old English *(ge)būr* and *geard*. The local pronunciation is 'broos-yard'.

Brundish *Burnedich* 1177, *Burnedis* 1204. 'The pasture on a stream', from Old English *burna* and *edisc*.

Brundon (near Sudbury) *Brandona* 1086 (Domesday Book), *Brandune* 1178. 'The hill where broom grows', from Old English *brōm* and *dūn*.

Bucklesham *Bukelesham* 1086 (Domesday Book), *Buclesham* 1286. 'The homestead or village of a man called *Buccel', from Old English *hām* and an Old English personal name. The local pronunciation is 'buckle-sh'm'.

Bulcamp (near Blythburgh) *Bulecampe* 1086 (Domesday Book), *Bulecamp* 13th century. 'The field or enclosure for bulls', from Old English *bula* and *camp*.

Bungay *Bongeia, Bunghea* 1086 (Domesday Book), *Bungeia* 1175. Probably 'the island at the raised neck of land', from an Old English word **bung* 'swelling, lump' and *ēg*. The first element would refer to the neck of the almost complete loop of the River Waveney where the early Norman castle stands on a mound at the heart of the town. The local pronunciation is 'bun-gee' (with a hard 'g').

Bunker's Hill (near Lound) A transferred name, one which occurs in several other English counties, commemorating the famous battle in the American War of Independence at Bunker Hill near Boston in 1775 at which the British General Howe defeated the colonial rebels, but at tremendous cost to his own forces.

Bures St Mary *Bure, Bura, Adbura* 1086 (Domesday Book), *Buras c.*1180, *Bures Seinte Marie* 1359. 'The dwellings or cottages', from Old English *būr* (plural *būras*). The affix St Mary, from the dedication of the church, distinguishes it from Mount Bures on the opposite bank of the River Stour in Essex (*Bures atte Munte* 1328, 'Bures at the mound or mount', from Middle English *munt*). The local pronunciation is 'bewers' or (sometimes) 'booers'.

Burgate Great & Little Green Marked thus on Hodskinson's map of 1783, named from *Burgata* 1086 (Domesday Book), *Burgate* 1254. 'The gate of, or at, the fortress or stronghold', from Old English *burh* and *geat*. The reference is to the ringwork fortification here (perhaps dating from the early 11th century).

Burgh *Burc, Burcg, Burh* 1086 (Domesday Book), *Burg* 1175. From Old English *burh* 'fortified place, stronghold'. The name refers to the banked enclosure and Roman villa site here. The local pronunciation is 'Burg' (with a hard 'g').

Burgh Castle (historically in Suffolk, transferred to Norfolk in the boundary change of 1974) *Burch* 1086 (Domesday Book), *Burc* 1168, *Borough-Castell* 1281. Identical in origin and meaning with the previous name. Here the reference is to the Roman fort of *Gariannonum*, built in the 3rd century and sited on the River Waveney where it is joined by the River Yare. The local pronunciation is 'Burra'.

Burstall *Burgestala* 1086 (Domesday Book), *Burcstal* 1194. From Old English *burh-stall* 'the site of a fort or stronghold'. The local pronunciation is 'burst'l'.

35

Bury St Edmunds *(on) Byrig c.*1035 (Anglo-Saxon will), *Sancte Eadmundes Byrig* 1038. 'The fortified town associated with St Ēadmund', from Old English *burh* (dative case *byrig*) and the name of the 9th century king of East Anglia who was killed by Danish Vikings in 869 and who quickly became revered as a martyr. His remains were brought in 870 to the small monastery here, hence the reference to *Sanctæ Eadmundes stow* 962-91 (in an 11th century copy of an Anglo-Saxon charter), 'the holy place of St Ēadmund', from Old English *stōw*. However the earlier name of the place was *Bæderices wirde* 945, *Beodrichesworth* 962 (in 13th century copies of Anglo-Saxon charters), *Beadriceswyrth c.*1030, 'the enclosed farmstead of a man called Beadurīc', from Old English *worth* and an Old English personal name. The local pronunciation is 'berry'.

Buss Creek (an arm of the River Blyth at Southwold) Marked thus on the Ordnance Survey map of 1837, probably from Middle English *bushe* (Old English *busc*) 'bush, thicket' with *creek*.

Butley *Butelea* 1086 (Domesday Book), *Buttele* 1195. Possibly 'the woodland clearing of a man called *Butta'*, from Old English *lēah* and an Old English personal name. Alternatively 'the clearing with tree-trunks or logs', from Old English **butt* (genitive case plural **butta*) and *lēah*. It gives its name to **Butley River** (marked thus on Hodskinson's map of 1783).

Buxhall *Bucyshealæ* 1000-2 (in an 11th century copy of an Anglo-Saxon will), *Buckeshala* 1086 (Domesday Book). 'The nook of land or hollow of the buck (male deer or he-goat)', from Old English *halh* and Old English *bucc*. However it is possible that the word *bucc* is used here as a personal name, thus 'the nook or hollow of a man called *Bucc'*. The local pronunciation is 'bucksawl'.

Buxlow Manor (in Knodishall) Named from *Buckeslawe* 1250, *Bukkeslowe* 1254. 'The mound or hill of the buck (male deer or he-goat)', from Old English *bucc* and *hlāw*. Here as in the previous name, the word *bucc* may be used as a personal name.

California (in Ipswich) A transferred name from the American state, here bestowed on an area of the town developed from the middle of the 19th century (the 282 plots made available in 1850 were allocated by ballot and eagerly taken up by the new landowners in scenes likened to the Californian gold rush of 1849).

In other instances of the name, a more ironical or whimsical sense is possible to describe a settlement considered poor or remote, and this may be appropriate for another example of **California** near Pettistree and also for one in Norfolk. The name California USA was originally a fictional one, for an island rich in gold and populated by Amazon-like women, that was then applied to the state.

Campsea Ashe (sometimes spelt Campsey Ash) *Campesche in Ashe* 1286, *Campese et Ahs* 1346, *Campsy Ash* 1674. This name combines the names of two originally separate places. Campsea is *Campeseia* in 1086 (Domesday Book), *Campeseye* 1254, 'the island, or dry ground in marsh, with a field or enclosure', from Old English *camp* and *ēg*. Ash(e) is *Esce* in 1086 (Domesday Book), *Eysse* 1249, '(the place at) the ash-tree(s)', from Old English *æsc*.

Capel St Andrew *Capeles* 1086 (Domesday Book), *Capele* 1316. '(The place at) the chapel', from Middle English (Old French) *capel*. The addition from the dedication of the church distinguishes it from the next name. The local pronunciation of both names is 'cayp'l'.

Capel St Mary *Capeles* 1254, *Capele* 1275. Identical in origin and meaning with the previous name, with distinguishing addition from the dedication of the church.

Carlton (near Saxmundham) *Carletuna* 1086 (Domesday Book), *Carleton* 1254. 'The farmstead or estate of the freemen or peasants', from Old Scandinavian *karl* (perhaps replacing Old English *ceorl*) and Old English *tūn*.

Carlton Colville *Karletun, Carletuna* 1086 (Domesday Book), *Carleton Colvile* 1346. Identical in origin and meaning with the previous name. The manorial addition is from the family of Robert *de Colevill*, here in 1230. The family took their name from Colleville in Normandy. Carlton (or Carleton) is a common place-name in all the old Danelaw areas of England, including East Anglia (besides the two Carltons in Suffolk, there are three examples of Carleton in Norfolk).

Cattawade *Cattiwad* 1247, *Cattiwade* 1256. 'The ford or crossing-place frequented by wildcats', from Old English *catt* (genitive case plural *catta*) and *(ge)wæd*. The reference is to an important crossing of the River Stour.

37

Cattishall *Catteshale* 1187, *Catteshal* 1238. Probably 'the nook of land belonging to a man called *Catt, or one frequented by wild-cats', from Old English *halh* with either an Old English personal name or Old English *catt*.

Cavendish *Kauanadisc* 1086 (Domesday Book), *Cavenedis* 1242. 'The enclosure or enclosed park of a man called *Cāfna', from an Old English personal name (genitive case *-an*) and Old English *edisc*.

Cavenham *Canauatham* [*sic*, for *Cauanatham*], *Kanauaham* [*sic*, for *Kauanaham*] 1086 (Domesday Book), *Cauenham* 1198. 'The homestead or village of a man called *Cāfna', from an Old English personal name and Old English *hām* (although the first Domesday form may suggest a personal name *Cāfnōth*). The local pronunciation is 'cav-n'm'.

Chadacre Park (near Hartest) *Chearteker* 1042-53 (in a 13th century copy of an Anglo-Saxon will), *Chardeker* 1275. 'The cultivated or arable land taken in from rough ground', from Old English *cert* 'patch of rough or wooded ground' and *æcer*. The river-name **Chad Brook** is a so-called back-formation from the place-name.

Chad Brook (a tributary of the River Stour), *see* Chadacre Park.

Chantry (in Ipswich) Modern estate named from The Chantry (marked *Chantry* on the Ordnance Survey map of 1805), a mansion house (now Sue Ryder Home) dating from the early 18th century.

Charsfield *Ceresfelda*, *Caresfelda* 1086 (Domesday Book), *Charesfeud* 1254. Old English *feld* 'tract of open land', possibly with a Celtic or pre-Celtic river-name *Cear* ('stony stream') as first element. A small tributary of the River Deben rises near here.

Chattisham *Cetessam* 1086 (Domesday Book), *Chettesham* 1190. Probably 'the homestead or village of a man called *Ceatt', from an Old English personal name and Old English *hām*.

Chedburgh *Cedeberia* 1086 (Domesday Book), *Cheddeberg* 1254. 'The hill or mound of a man called Cedda', from an Old English personal name and Old English *beorg*. The local pronunciation is 'chedbruh'.

Chediston *Cidestan, Cedestan* 1086 (Domesday Book), *Chedestan* 12th century. 'The stone of a man called Cedd', from an Old English personal name and Old English *stān*. There is a Roman villa site here, but the 'stone' of the name probably refers to one or other of the massive erratic glacial stones found in the vicinity (one of which may have been a preaching stone dedicated to or commemorating the famous *Cedd*, first bishop of the East Saxons, who died in 664). The local pronunciation is 'cheddis-t'n' or (sometimes) 'cheston'.

Chelmondiston *Chelmundeston* 1174, *Chelmondeston* 1219. 'The farmstead or estate of a man called Cēolmund', from an Old English personal name and *tūn*. The local pronunciation is 'chelms-t'n' or 'chelmondis-t'n' (with the stress on the third syllable).

Chelsworth *Ceorleswyrthe* 962 (Anglo-Saxon charter), *Cæorlesweorth* 962-91, *Ceorlesweorth* 1000-2 (in 11th century copies of Anglo-Saxon wills), *Cerleswrda* 1086 (Domesday Book). 'The enclosure, or enclosed farmstead, of the freeman or of a man called Ceorl', from Old English *worth* and either Old English *ceorl* or the Old English personal name from this word. A noteworthy feature of the 962 charter is that it contains a full description of the bounds of Chelsworth at that date.

Chevington *Ceuentuna* 1086 (Domesday Book), *Cheventon* 1254. 'The farmstead or estate of a man called Ceofa', from an Old English personal name (genitive case -*an*) and Old English *tūn*.

Chickering *Chikeringe c.*946 (in a 13th century copy of an Anglo-Saxon will), *Ciccheling, Cikelinga* 1086 (Domesday Book). Possibly '(the settlement of) the family or followers of a man called *Ciccel*, from an Old English personal name and -*ingas*.

Chillesford *Cesefortda* [*sic*] 1086 (Domesday Book), *Chiselford* 1211. 'The gravel ford', from Old English *ceosol* and *ford*. There is a crossing of Butley River here. The local pronunciation is 'chillz-f'd' or 'chillers-f'd'.

Chilton (near Sudbury) *Ciltona* 1086 (Domesday Book), *Chiltune c.*1180. 'The farmstead or estate of the young (noble)men', from Old English *cild* (genitive case plural *cilda*) and *tūn*.

Chilton Hall (near Stowmarket) *Ciltuna* 1086 (Domesday Book), *Chilton* 1346. Identical in origin and meaning with the previous name.

Chilton Street (near Clare) *Chilton* 1254, 1316. Identical in origin and meaning with the previous names, with the late addition of *street* in the sense 'hamlet'.

Chippenhall Green (near Cratfield) *Cibbehala, Cebbenhala* 1086 (Domesday Book), *Chebenhale* 12th century. 'The nook of land or hollow of a man called Ceobba', from an Old English personal name (genitive case *-an*) and Old English *halh*.

Clare *Clara* 1086 (Domesday Book), *Clare* 1198. Probably from a Latin stream-name *Clāra* 'the clear one'. A small stream (actually recorded as *Clarus* 'from the cleernes of the streame' in 1618) flows south from Chilton Street into the River Stour here.

Claydon *Clainduna* 1086 (Domesday Book), *Cleidun* 1198. 'The clayey hill', from Old English *clǣgig* (dative case *clǣgigan*) and *dūn*.

Clopton (near Otley) *Clop(e)tuna* 1086 (Domesday Book), *Clopton* 1186. 'The farmstead or estate by or on a hill or hills', from Old English **clopp(a)* and *tūn*. **Clopton Corner** is so named from the sharp bend in the main road here.

Clopton Green (near Wickhambrook) Marked as *Clapton Green* on Hodskinson's map of 1783 and on the Ordnance Survey map of 1836, identical in origin and meaning with the previous name.

Cockfield *Cokefeld* 946-c.951 (in a 13th century copy of an Anglo-Saxon will), *Cohhanfeldæa, Cochanfelde* 962-91 (in an 11th century copy of an Anglo-Saxon will), *Cothefelda* [*sic*, for *Cochefelda*] 1086 (Domesday Book). 'The open land of a man called *Cohha', from an Old English personal name (genitive case *-an*) and *feld*.

Coddenham *Code(n)ham* 1086 (Domesday Book), *Codeneham* 12th century. 'The homestead or village of a man called *Cod(d)a', from an Old English personal name (genitive case *-an*) and *hām*.

Coldfair Green (near Knodishall) Marked as *Cold Fair Green* on the Ordnance Survey map of 1837, but *Coldford Green* on Hodskinson's map of 1783, thus probably 'the cold ford', with reference to a crossing of Hundred River. The current form of the name is no doubt partly the result of popular etymology (fairs are in fact recorded as being held here at an early date).

Combs *Cambas* 1086 (Domesday Book), *Cambes* 1130. 'The hill-crests or ridges', from Old English *camb* (plural *cambas*). The local pronunciation is 'cooms'.

Coney Weston *Cunegestone* 1051-7 (in a 13th century copy of an Anglo-Saxon writ), *Cunegestuna* 1086 (Domesday Book), *Cunewestone* 1254. 'The king's manor, the royal estate', from Old Scandinavian *konungr* and Old English *tūn*. The later development of the name has been influenced by nearby Market Weston and by the word *coney* (Middle English *coni*) 'a rabbit'.

Conyer's Green (near Great Barton) Marked thus on the Ordnance Survey map of 1837, but *Conyard Green* on Hodskinson's map of 1783, probably from Middle English *coninger* 'a rabbit-warren'. Rabbits were widely bred for both their fur and for food from medieval times onwards.

Cookley *Cokelei* 1086 (Domesday Book), *Kukeleia* late 12th century. Possibly 'the wood or woodland clearing of a man called *Cuca', from an Old English personal name and *lēah*. Alternatively the first element may rather be an Old English *cucu* 'the cuckoo' (*compare* Yaxley which contains another old word for this bird).

Copdock *Coppedoc* 1195, *Coppedac* 1254. 'The pollarded oak-tree, i.e. the oak-tree with its top removed', from Old English *coppod* and *āc*. There must have been a very prominent tree at the road junction here on the important north-south route (a former Roman road).

Cornard, Great & Little *Corn(i)erda* 1086 (Domesday Book), *Cornerth* 1196, *Cornherth Magna*, *-Parva* 1254. 'The cultivated land used for growing corn', from Old English *corn* and *erth*. The early affixes are Latin *magna* 'great' and *parva* 'little'.

Corton *Karetuna* 1086 (Domesday Book), *Korton* 1235. 'The farmstead or estate of a man called Kári', from an Old Scandinavian personal name and Old English *tūn*.

Cosford (district, earlier the name of a medieval Hundred) *Corsforde* 1086 (Domesday Book), *Corsford* 1206. 'The ford by the marsh or fen', from Celtic **cors* and Old English *ford*. This was a crossing of the River Brett (now Cosford Bridge) where the Hundred meetings were no doubt once held.

Cotton *Codetuna, Kodetun* 1086 (Domesday Book), *Cotton* 1203. 'The farmstead or estate of a man called Coda', from Old English *tūn* and an Old English personal name.

Cove, North *Cove* 1204, *North Cove* 1285. From Old English *cofa* which had various senses such as 'hut, shelter, den' as well as 'recess, hollow, cove': the reference here is uncertain. The local pronunciation is 'coov'. The affix *North* distinguishes it from South Cove which lies some five miles south east.

Cove, South *Coua* 1086 (Domesday Book), *Suth Cove* 1327. Named from the same Old English word as North Cove, but here possibly with reference to a former cove or other coastal feature. *South* to distinguish it from North Cove.

Covehithe *Coofythe* 1523, *Coveheyth alias Northales* 1524. 'The harbour near (South) Cove', from Old English *hȳth*. The original name of this place was *Nor(t)hals, Northala, Nordhalla* 1086 (Domesday Book), *Northales* 1254, either 'the northern nooks of land', or 'the northern spit of land', from Old English *north* with either *halh* (plural *halas*) or *hals*.

Cowlinge *Culinge* 1086 (Domesday Book), *Culinges* 1195. Probably 'the place associated with a man called *Cul or *Cula', from an Old English personal name with the suffix *-ing* (dative case *-inge*), although some early spellings suggest '(the settlement of) *Cul(a)'s family or followers', with the plural suffix *-ingas* 'people of'. The local pronunciation is 'coolinj'.

Cranley *Cranlea* 1086 (Domesday Book), *Cranele* 1198. 'The woodland clearing frequented by cranes or herons', from Old English *cran* (genitive case plural *crana*) and *lēah*.

Cransford *Crane(s)forda* 1086 (Domesday Book), *Crane(s)ford* 13th century. 'The ford frequented by cranes or herons', from Old English *cran* and *ford*. There is a crossing of the River Alde near here.

Cratfield *Cratafelda* 1086 (Domesday Book), *Cratefeld* 1165. 'The open land of a man called *Crǣta', from Old English *feld* and an Old English personal name.

Creeting St Mary & St Peter *Cratingas, Cratingis* 1086 (Domesday Book), *Creting Sancte Marie, Creting Sancti Petri* 1254. '(The settlement of) the family or followers of a man called *Crǣta', from an Old English personal name and *-ingas*. The distinguishing affixes are from the dedications of the churches.

Cretingham *Gretingaham, Gratingeham* 1086 (Domesday Book), *Gretingham* 1195. 'The homestead or village of the people from a gravelly district', from Old English *grēot* with *-inga-* (genitive case of *-ingas* 'people of') and *hām*. Spellings with *Cret-* (perhaps influenced by Creeting) first appear in the 14th century.

Crowfield *Crofelda* 1086 (Domesday Book), *Croffeld* c.1230. Probably 'the open land by the nook or corner', from Old English **crōh* and *feld*. Spellings with *Crowe-* (where the rare first element has been influenced by the common word *crow*) first appear in the 15th century.

Culford *Culeford, Coleford* c.1040 (Anglo-Saxon charter), *Culeforda* 1086 (Domesday Book). 'The ford of a man called *Cula', from an Old English personal name and Old English *ford*. The ford was no doubt a crossing of the River Lark.

Culpho *Culfole* [*sic*] 1086 (Domesday Book), *Colfho* 1168, *Culfho* 1178. The second element is Old English *hōh* 'a spur of land, a hill-spur', the first may be the Old English personal name *Cūthwulf* in reduced form or an unknown word.

Dagworth (near Haughley) *Dagaworda* 1086 (Domesday Book), *Daggewurthe* 1218. 'The enclosure or enclosed farmstead of a man called *Dagga', from Old English *worth* and an Old English personal name.

Dalham *Dalham* 1086 (Domesday Book), 1200. 'The homestead or village in a valley', from Old English *dæl* and *hām*. The valley is that of the River Kennet (referred to as *the ryver of Dale* in 1618, a back-formation from the place-name).

Dallinghoo *Dallingahou, Delingahou* 1086 (Domesday Book), *Dalingeho c.*1150. 'The hill-spur of the family or followers of a man called D(e)alla', from an Old English personal name with *-inga-* (genitive case of *-ingas* 'people of') and *hōh*.

Darmsden *Dermodesduna* 1086 (Domesday Book), *Dermondesdoune* 1307. 'The hill of a man called Dēormōd', from Old English *dūn* and an Old English personal name.

Darsham *Dersham, Diresham* 1086 (Domesday Book), *Dersham* 1224. 'The homestead or village of a man called Dēor', from an Old English personal name and *hām*.

Debach *Depebecs, Depebek, Debenbeis* 1086 (Domesday Book), *Debech* 1201. 'The valley or ridge near the river called *Dēope* (the deep one)', from an Old English river-name (*see* Debenham) and either *bece* or *bæc* (dative case **bece*). A small tributary of the River Deben (which may have shared its name in early times) flows just to the north of here. The local pronunciation is 'debbich'.

Deben, River Recorded as *Deue* 1577, *Deane* 1618, *Deben* 1735, *see* Debenham. The local pronunciation is 'deeb'n' (thus contrasting with that of the village).

Debenham *Debham* 1042-66 (in a 12th century copy of an Anglo-Saxon charter), *Depbenham, Depham* 1086 (Domesday Book), *Debenham* 1226. 'The homestead or village by the river called *Dēope* (the deep one, or the stream in a deep valley)', from an Old English river-name and *hām*. The river referred to is the **Deben**, this name being a relatively late back-formation from the place-name. The local pronunciation is 'debben'm'.

Denham (near Bury St Edmunds) *Denham* 1086 (Domesday Book), 1254. 'The homestead or village in a valley', from Old English *denu* and *hām*.

Denham (near Eye) *Denham* 1086 (Domesday Book), 1212. Identical in origin and meaning with the previous name.

Dennington *Dingifetuna, Dingiuetona* 1086 (Domesday Book), *Dingieueton* 1169. 'The farmstead or estate of a woman called **Denegifu*', from an Old English personal name and *tūn*. This is one of the four Suffolk places named from an Anglo-Saxon female landowner.

Denston *Danerdestuna*, *Danardestuna* 1086 (Domesday Book), *Denardeston* 1220. 'The farmstead or estate of a man called Deneheard', from an Old English personal name and *tūn*.

Depden (Green) *Depdana* 1086 (Domesday Book), *Depedene* 1198. 'The deep valley', from Old English *dēop* and *denu*, with the later addition of *green* 'village green, hamlet'. Land above the village is among the highest in Suffolk.

Dodnash Wood & Priory Farm (in Bentley) Recorded as *Dodnash Wood*, *Dodnash House or Priory* on Hodskinson's map of 1783, and as *Dodneis Wood*, *Great Dodneis Farm* on the Ordnance Survey map of 1805, named from *Todenes* [*sic*] 1086 (Domesday Book), *Dodenessa* 1188, *Dodeneis* 1254, 'the ash-tree of a man called Dodda', from an Old English personal name (genitive case -*an*) and *æsc*. There was once an Augustinian priory here, founded in the 12th century.

Dove, River Earlier called simply *Eie* in 1577 (from the town of Eye past which it flows), so *Dove* is probably a late whimsical name from the bird on the analogy of other Suffolk stream-names like Lark, Linnet and Wren.

Downham, Santon *Dunham* 1086 (Domesday Book), *Dounham* 1277. 'The homestead or village on or near a hill', from Old English *dūn* and *hām*, with the addition *Santon* from its proximity to Santon in Norfolk (*Santuna* 1086 Domesday Book, *Santona* 1121), 'the farmstead or estate with sandy soil', from Old English *sand* and *tūn*.

Drinkstone *Drincestune* 1042-66 (in a 12th century copy of an Anglo-Saxon charter), *Drencestuna*, *Drincestona* 1086 (Domesday Book). 'The farmstead or estate of a man called Drengr', from an Old Scandinavian personal name and Old English *tūn*. The local pronunciation is 'drinks-t'n'.

Dublin (near Occold) No doubt a transferred name from the Irish capital city, *compare* Little London.

Dunningworth Hall (near Blaxhall) Marked thus on the Ordnance Survey map of 1837, and on Hodskinson's map of 1783, named from Dunningworth, *Duniworda* 1086 (Domesday Book), *Dunningewurtha* 1177, 'the enclosed farmstead of the family or followers of a man called Dunn(a)', from an Old English personal name with -*inga*- (genitive case of -*ingas* 'people of') and *worth*.

Dunwich *Duneuuic* 1086 (Domesday Book), *Dunewich* 12th century. Probably 'the harbour or trading centre at the low hills or dunes', from Old English *dūn* (genitive case plural *dūna*) and *wīc*. An earlier identification of this place with the Celtic name *Domnoc*, mentioned in Bede's Ecclesiastical History (*c*.731) as the site of the first episcopal see of the East Angles established by St Felix, is doubtful: it is much more likely that the reference is to the Roman fort (*Burg*) at Walton near Felixstowe. The local pronunciation is 'dunnidge' or 'dunnitch'.

Earl Soham, *see* Soham.

Earl Stonham, *see* Stonham.

East Bergholt, *see* Bergholt.

East Bridge (near Theberton) Marked thus on the Ordnance Survey map of 1837, and as *East Bridge Street* on Hodskinson's map of 1783, earlier *Briges* 1086 (Domesday Book), *Brigge* 1275, '(the place at) the bridge', from Old English *brycg*. This hamlet is at a crossing of Minsmere River east of Theberton.

Easton *Estuna* 1086 (Domesday Book), *Eston* 1219. 'The east farmstead or estate', from Old English *ēast* and *tūn*. Perhaps named in relation to Monewden. The same name occurs twice in Suffolk (*see* next name) and is found in most English counties.

Easton Bavents (near Southwold) *Estuna* 1086 (Domesday Book), *Eston Bavent* 1330. Identical in origin and meaning with the previous name. The distinguishing affix is manorial, from the family of Thomas *de Bavent*, here in 1316. The family took their name from Bavent near Caen in Normandy.

Edwardstone *Eduardestuna* 1086 (Domesday Book), *Edwardiston* 1327. 'The farmstead or estate of a man called Ēadweard', from an Old English personal name and *tūn*. The local pronunciation is 'edwards-t'n'.

Eleigh, Brent & Monks *Illeyge* 946-*c*.951 (in a 13th century copy of an Anglo-Saxon will), *Illanlege* 1000-1002 (in an 11th century copy of an Anglo-Saxon will), *Illeleia, Ilelega* 1086 (Domesday Book), *Brendeylleye* 1312, *Monekesillegh* 1304, *Illeghe Combust, Illeghe Monacorum* 1327. 'The woodland clearing of a man called *Illa', from an Old English personal name

46

and *lēah*. The distinguishing affixes are from Middle English *brend* and *combust* 'burnt, destroyed by fire' (no doubt alluding to some early conflagration in the village) and Middle English *mon(e)ke*, Latin *monachus* 'a monk' (alluding to early possession of this estate by the monks of Christ Church, Canterbury). The local pronunciation is 'eeli'.

Ellough   *Elga* 1086 (Domesday Book), *Elgh* 1286. Etymology uncertain, but possibly '(the place at) the heathen temple', from Old English *ealh* (dative case **ealge*). The local pronunciation is 'ellow' or 'ella'.

Elmham, South   *Almeham, Elmeham* 1086 (Domesday Book), *Elmham* 12th century, *Suthelmeham* 1252. 'The homestead or village where elm-trees grow', from Old English *elm* and *hām*. *South* to distinguish it from North Elmham in Norfolk. The parishes of **All Saints South Elmham** (*All Seyntes* 1524), **St James South Elmham** (*Seynt Jamys* 1524), **St Margaret South Elmham** (*Seynt Margarettes* 1524), and **St Michael South Elmham** (*Seynt Mighelles* 1524) are distinguished by the dedications of their churches. However **St Cross South Elmham** (*St George Southelmham* on Hodskinson's map of 1783 and *Sancroft or St George Southelmham* on the Ordnance Survey map of 1837) has its affix from *Sancroft* 1254, *Sandcroft* 1391, 'the sandy croft or enclosure', from Old English *sand* and *croft*, so that here *St Cross* is the result of popular etymology. The local pronunciation is 'elm'm'.

Elmsett   *Ylmesæton* 962-91 (in an 11th century copy of an Anglo-Saxon will), *Elmeseta* 1086 (Domesday Book). Probably '(the settlement of) the dwellers among the elm-trees', from Old English **elme* and *sæte*.

Elmswell   *Elmeswella* 1086 (Domesday Book), *Elmeswell* 1200. 'The spring or stream where elm-trees grow', from Old English *elm* and *wella*.

Elveden   *Eluedena, Heluedana* 1086 (Domesday Book), *Elueden* 1179. Probably 'the valley haunted by elves or fairies', from Old English *elf* (genitive plural *elfa*) and *denu*. Alternatively this may be 'the swan valley' with a first element Old English *elfitu* 'swan'.

Eriswell   *Hereswella* 1086 (Domesday Book), *Ereswell* 1183. Probably 'the spring or stream of a man called Her or *Heri', from an Old English personal name and *wella*.

47

Erwarton *Eurewardestuna* 1086 (Domesday Book), *Euerewardeston* 1196. 'The farmstead or estate of a man called *Eoforweard', from an Old English personal name and *tūn*. The local pronunciation is 'erwor-t'n' (with the stress on the second syllable).

Euston *Euestuna* 1086 (Domesday Book), *Euuestun* c.1095. 'The farmstead or estate of a man called Efi', from an Old English personal name and *tūn*. The rare personal name has been identified as that of a moneyer who struck coins for the East Anglian kings in the mid-8th century.

Exning *Essellinge* [*sic*] 1086 (Domesday Book), *Ixninges, Exningis* 1158. '(The settlement of) the family or followers of a man called *Gyxen', from an Old English personal name and *-ingas*.

Eye *Eia* 1086 (Domesday Book), *Eye* 1103. '(The place at) the island (of dry or higher ground in a marshy area)', from Old English *ēg*.

Eyke *Eik* 1185, *Eyk* 1270. '(The place at) the oak-tree', from Old Scandinavian *eik*. There is ancient woodland including oaks at nearby Staverton Park. The local pronunciation is 'ike'.

Fakenham Magna & Little Fakenham *Fakenham* c.1060, *Fachenham, Litla Fachenham* 1086 (Domesday Book), *Fakenham Magna, -Parva* 1254. 'The homestead or village of a man called *Facca', from Old English *hām* and an Old English personal name (genitive case *-an*). The distinguishing affixes are Latin *magna* 'great' and *parva* 'little'. The local pronunciation is 'fayk-n'm'. Fakenham in Norfolk is identical in origin and meaning.

Falkenham *Faltenham* 1086 (Domesday Book), 1291. Probably 'the homestead or village of a man called *Falta', from an Old English personal name (genitive case *-an*) and *hām*. The change from *Falt-* to *Falk-* is early (from 1200), but spellings with *Falt-* occur as late as the 17th century. The local pronunciation is 'follk-n'm'.

Farnham *Farnham, Ferneham* 1086 (Domesday Book), *Farnham* 1206. 'The homestead or enclosure where ferns grow', from Old English *fearn* and either *hām* or *hamm*. Farnham in Essex is identical in origin and meaning.

Felixstowe *Filchestou* 1254, *Filchestowe* 1291. Probably 'the holy place or assembly place of a man called *Filica', from Old English *stōw* and an Old English personal name. The personal name is probably an anglicization of (St) Felix, first Bishop of East Anglia (*c*.630-648), with whom of course the place is associated (*see* below). The current form of the place-name does not appear until the early 16th century. The earlier name for the original site of the town (**Old Felixstowe**) was *Burch, Burg* in 1086 (Domesday Book), 'the fortress or stronghold', from Old English *burh*, with reference to the Roman fort (later known as *Walton Castle* when it was re-fortified in the 12th century) which, until it was washed away by the encroaching sea, guarded the estuaries of the Deben and the Orwell, *see* Walton. It is most probable that this same fort is to be identified with *Domnoc* (a Celtic name, previously interpreted as 'the deep place' but more likely to be 'the church building' from a Celtic borrowing of Late Latin *dominicum*), mentioned in Bede's Ecclesiastical History (*c*.731) as the site where St Felix established his see (the church at Walton is dedicated to St Felix).

Felsham *Fealsham* 1086 (Domesday Book), *Felesham c*.1095. 'The homestead or village of a man called *Fæli', from Old English *hām* and an Old English personal name.

Finborough, Great & Little *Fineberga* 1086 (Domesday Book), *Parva Fineberg* 1226-8, *Fineberg Magna* 1254. Possibly 'the hill or mound frequented by the woodpecker', from Old English *fina* and *beorg*. Alternatively 'the hill or mound of a man called *Fīna', from the same word used as a personal name. The early affixes are Latin *magna* 'great' and *parva* 'little'. The local pronunciation is 'finbruh'.

Fingal Street (near Worlingworth) Marked as *Fincle Street* on the Ordnance Survey map of 1837, probably from Middle English *fen(e)kel* 'fennel', a plant widely used in medieval and later times for medicinal purposes, specifically as a cure for abdominal pain and wind. *Street* has the sense 'hamlet'.

Finningham *Finingaham* 1086 (Domesday Book), *Finingeham* 1191. 'The homestead of the family or followers of a man called *Fīna', from an Old English personal name with *-inga-* (genitive case of *-ingas* 'people of') and *hām*.

Flempton *Flemingtuna* 1086 (Domesday Book), *Fleminton* 1197. Probably 'the farmstead or estate of the Fleming or Flemings (people from Flanders)', from Old English *Fleming* and *tūn*.

Flixton (near Bungay) *Flixtuna* 1086 (Domesday Book), *Flixton* 1254. 'The farmstead or estate of a man called Flík or Flikkr', from Old English *tūn* and an Old Scandinavian personal name.

Flixton (near Lowestoft) *Flixtuna* 1086 (Domesday Book), *Flixton* 1254. Identical in origin and meaning with the previous name.

Flowton *Flochetuna* 1086 (Domesday Book), *Floketon* 1201. 'The farmstead or estate of a man called Flóki', from Old English *tūn* and an Old Scandinavian personal name. The local pronunciation is 'flow-t'n'.

Fordley (near Middleton) *Forle* 1086 (Domesday Book), *Fordle* 1254, *Fordley* 1783, *Middleton cum Fordley* 1837 (Ordnance Survey map). 'The woodland clearing by a ford', from Old English *ford* and *lēah*. The ford was a crossing of a tributary of Minsmere River.

Forest Heath (district), a modern name, referring to the local topography.

Fornham All Saints, St Genevieve & St Martin *Fornham, Genonefæforham* [*sic*, for *Genouefæ-*] 1086 (Domesday Book), *Fornham Omnium Sanctorum*, *Fornham Sancti Martini* 1254. 'The homestead or village where trout are caught', from Old English *forne* and *hām*. The Fornhams lie on both sides of the River Lark. The distinguishing affixes are from the dedications of the churches.

Forward Green (near Earl Stonham). Marked thus on Hodskinson's map of 1783 and on the Ordnance Survey map of 1837, from the ModE adjective *forward* in the sense 'near or in front', with reference to the position of this *green* 'village green, hamlet' relative to Earl Stonham.

Foxhall Hall & Heath (near Kesgrave) Marked thus on the Ordnance Survey map of 1805, and as *Foxhall (Heath)* on Hodkinson's map of 1783, named from *Foxehola* 1086 (Domesday Book), *Foxhole* 1254, 'the fox-hole, the fox's earth', from Old English *fox-hol*.

Framlingham *Fram(e)lingaham* 1086 (Domesday Book), *Framillingeham* 1175. 'The homestead of the family or followers of a man called *Framela', from an Old English personal name with *-inga-* (genitive case of *-ingas* 'people of') and *hām*.

Framsden *Framesdena* 1086 (Domesday Book), *Framesden* 1213. 'The valley of a man called Fram', from Old English *denu* and an Old English personal name.

Freckenham *Frekeham* 895 (in a 12th century copy of an Anglo-Saxon charter), *Frakenaham* 1086 (Domesday Book), *Frekenham* 1225. 'The homestead or village of the warrior, or of a man called *Freca', from Old English *freca* or a personal name from that word (genitive case *-an*) and Old English *hām*. The Domesday Book spelling suggests rather 'the homestead of the warriors', from the genitive case plural *frecena*. The local pronunciation is 'frek-n'm'.

Fressingfield *Fessefelda* [*sic*] 1086 (Domesday Book), *Frisingefeld* 1185. Possibly 'the open land of the family or followers of a man called Frīsa (the Frisian)', from an Old English personal name with *-inga-* (genitive case of *-ingas* 'people of') and *feld*.

Freston *Fresantun* 1000-2 (in an 11th century copy of an Anglo-Saxon will), *Fresetuna* 1086 (Domesday Book). 'The farmstead or estate of the Frisian', from Old English *Frēsa* (genitive case *-an*, possibly used as a personal name) and *tūn*.

Friday Street (near Brandeston) Marked thus on the Ordnance Survey map of 1837. There are other instances of this name in Suffolk (e.g. at West Row) and in other counties, and the allusion to *Friday* may be linked with the medieval superstitions regarding this day of the week (through its association with the Crucifixion and with fasting), thus perhaps referring to a street or hamlet that was poverty-stricken, or even to one near the site of the local gallows.

Friston *Frisetuna* 1086 (Domesday Book), *Freston* 1254. 'The farmstead or estate of the Frisians', from the Old English folk-name *Frīsa*, *Frēsa* (here probably a genitive plural form) and *tūn*.

Fritton (historically in Suffolk, transferred to Norfolk in the boundary change of 1974) *Fridetuna* 1086 (Domesday Book), *Freton* 1224. Possibly 'the farmstead or estate offering safety or protection', from Old English *frith* and *tūn*. Alternatively, 'the farmstead or estate of a man called Frithi', from *tūn* and an Old Scandinavian personal name. Fritton near Morningthorpe in Norfolk is identical in origin and meaning.

Frostenden *Froxedena* 1086 (Domesday Book), *Frosteden* 1242. Probably 'the valley frequented by frogs', from Old English *frosc, frox* (genitive plural *frosca, froxa*) and *denu*. The local pronunciation is 'fross'n-d'n'.

Fynn, River (a tributary of the River Deben) Marked as *The Finn River* and as *River Fyn* on the Ordnance Survey map of 1805, probably a so-called back-formation from *Finnford Bridge* (at Witnesham, marked thus on the 1837 Ordnance Survey map), which is possibly to be identified with *Finesforda* 1086 (Domesday Book), 'the ford of a man called Finn', from Old English *ford* and an Old Scandinavian personal name.

Gazeley *Gaysle* 1219, *Gaisle* 1254. 'The woodland clearing of a man called *Gǣgi*', from Old English *lēah* and an Old English personal name (genitive case *Gǣges*).

Gedding *Gedinga* 1086 (Domesday Book), *Geddinges* 12th century. '(The settlement of) the family or followers of a man called *Gydda*', from an Old English personal name and *-ingas*.

Gedgrave (near Orford) *Gatagraua, Gategraua* 1086 (Domesday Book), *Gategrave* 1275, *Gategraue* 1327. 'The grove or copse where goats are kept', from Old English *gāt* (genitive plural *gāta*) and *grāf(a)*.

Gibraltar (near Swilland) A transferred name from the British territory on the southern coast of Spain, usually given to a spot considered to be rather remote. There are examples of the name in several other English counties, one of them being that of a village on the Lincolnshire coast.

Gipping *Gippinges* 1154-89, *Gypping, Gippingneweton* c.1290. '(The settlement of) the family or followers of a man called Gyppi or *Gyppa*', from an Old English personal name with *-ingas*. The early addition *Neweton* refers to nearby Old Newton. The river-name **Gipping** (recorded from 1586) is a so-called back-formation from the place-name.

Gisleham *Gisleham* 1086 (Domesday Book), *Giselham* 1203. 'The homestead or village of a man called *Gysla', from Old English *hām* and an Old English personal name. The local pronunciation is 'gizzl'm'.

Gislingham *Gyselingham* 1043-7 (in a 13th century copy of an Anglo-Saxon document), *Gislingaham, Gissilincham* 1086 (Domesday Book). 'The homestead or village of the family or followers of a man called *Gysla', from an Old English personal name with *-inga-* (genitive case of *-ingas* 'people of') and *hām*. The local pronunciation is 'gizzling'm'.

Glem, River There are two Suffolk rivers so named, *see* Glemham and Glemsford.

Glemham, Great & Little *Glaimham, Gl(i)emham* 1086 (Domesday Book), *Parva Glemham* 1254, *Magna Glemham* 1336. Probably 'the homestead or village noted for its revelry or games', from Old English *glēam* and *hām*. The early affixes are Latin *magna* 'great' and *parva* 'little'. The river-name **Glem** (recorded as *Gleme* in 1577 and 1618, a tributary of the Alde) is a so-called back-formation from the place-name.

Glemsford *Glemesford* 1042-66 (in a 12th century copy of an Anglo-Saxon charter), *Clamesforda* [*sic*] 1086 (Domesday Book). Probably 'the ford where people assemble for revelry or games', from Old English *glēam* and *ford*. The river-name **Glem** (a tributary of the River Stour) is a so-called back-formation from the place-name.

Glevering Hall (Farm) (near Wickham Market) *Glereuinges* 1086 (Domesday Book), *Gleringes* 1206, *Gleueringge* 1327. Possibly '(the settlement of) the family or followers of a man called *Glēawfrith', from an Old English personal name and *-ingas*.

Gosbeck *Gosebech* 1179, *Gosebec* 1212. 'The stream frequented by geese', from Old English *gōs* and *bece* (replaced or influenced by Old Scandinavian *bekkr*).

Greenstreet Green (near Great Bricett) Marked as *Green Street Green* on Hodskinson's map of 1783 and on the Ordnance Survey map of 1837, 'the green or grassy hamlet', from *green* (adjective) and *street*, with the addition of *green* (noun) 'village green'.

53

Grimston Hall (near Trimley St Martin) Marked thus on Hodskinson's map of 1783 and on the Ordnance Survey map of 1805, named from *Grimestuna* 1086 (Domesday Book), *Grymeston* 1327, 'the farmstead or estate of a man called Grímr', from Old English *tūn* and an Old Scandinavian personal name. **Grimstone End** near Pakenham, recorded as *Grimstuna c*.1200, has the same origin and meaning, as indeed have the Grimston names in Essex and other counties. The personal name *Grímr* (Old English *Grīm*) was originally a byname for the chief Germanic heathen god Odin or Woden, later equated with the Devil, so that some of these Grimston(e) names may have had a derogatory sense for settlements in a poor situation or considered to be haunted.

Groton *Grotena* 1086 (Domesday Book), *Grotene* 1201. Probably 'the sandy or gravelly stream', from Old English **groten* and *ēa*. The local pronunciation is 'grow-t'n'.

Grundisburgh *Grundesburc(h)* 1086 (Domesday Book), *Grundesburg* 1235. Possibly 'the stronghold or fortified manor of a man called *Grund', from Old English *burh* and an Old English personal name. Alternatively the first element may rather be Old English *grund* 'ground, foundation' (perhaps in particular referring to the foundation of ancient buildings at a Romano-British site such as that in the neighbouring parish of Burgh). The local pronunciation is 'grundsbruh' or 'grunsbruh'.

Gull, The (a feeder of River Yox) From dialect *gull* (Middle English *go(u)le*) 'a channel, a watercourse'. There are other examples of this stream-name, among them one near Otley and another near Debenham.

Gunton *Guniton* 1184, *Guneton* 1198. 'The farmstead or estate of a man called Gunni', from Old English *tūn* and an Old Scandinavian personal name (genitive case *Gunna*). Gunton in Norfolk is identical in origin and meaning.

Hacheston *Hacestuna, Hece(s)tuna* 1086 (Domesday Book), *Hascheton* 1197. 'The farmstead or estate of a man called Hæcci', from Old English *tūn* and an Old English personal name. The local pronunciation is 'hatches-t'n'.

Hadleigh *Hedlæge, Hædleage* 962-91 (in an 11th century copy of an Anglo-Saxon will), *Hæthleh* 1042-66 (Anglo-Saxon charter), *Hetlega* 1086 (Domesday Book). 'The heath clearing, the woodland clearing where heather grows', from

Old English *hǣth* and *lēah*. The local pronunciation is 'hadlee'. Hadleigh in Essex is identical in origin and meaning.

Halesworth *Healesuurda, Halesuuorda* 1086 (Domesday Book), *Haleswurde* 1195. Probably 'the enclosure or enclosed farmstead of a man called *Hæle', from Old English *worth* and an Old English personal name. The local pronunciation is often 'harls-w'th'.

Hardwick Manor (south of Bury St Edmunds) Marked as *Hardwick(e) House* on Hodskinson's map of 1783 and on the Ordnance Survey map of 1805, named from *Herdewic c.*1130, 'the herd farm, the farm for livestock', from Old English *heorde-wīc*.

Hargrave *Haragraua* 1086 (Domesday Book), *Haregraue c.*1150. Probably 'the hoar or grey wood or copse', from Old English *hār* and *grāf(a)*. Alternatively 'the wood frequented by hares' if the first element is rather Old English *hara* 'a hare'.

Harkstead *Herchesteda* 1086 (Domesday Book), *Herkestede* 1198. Probably 'the pasture or homestead of a man called Hereca', from Old English *stede* and an Old English personal name.

Harleston *Heroluestuna* 1086 (Domesday Book), *Herleston* 1197. 'The farmstead or estate of a man called Heoruwulf or Herewulf', from Old English *tūn* and an Old English personal name. The local pronunciation is 'harls-t'n'.

Hartest *Hertest* 1042-66 (in a 12th century copy of an Anglo-Saxon charter), *Herte(r)st* 1086 (Domesday Book). 'The wooded hill frequented by harts or stags', from Old English *heorot* and *hyrst*.

Hasketon *Hascetuna, Haschetuna* 1086 (Domesday Book), *Hasketone* 1254. 'The farmstead or estate of a man called *Haseca', from Old English *tūn* and an Old English personal name.

Haughley *Hagele* 1035-44 (in a 13th century copy of an Anglo-Saxon will), *Hagala* 1086 (Domesday Book). 'The wood or woodland clearing with a hedge, or where hawthorns grow', from Old English *haga* and *lēah*. The local pronunciation is 'hawlee'. **Haughley Green** is *Hawleigh Green* on Hodskinson's map of 1783, from *green* 'village green, hamlet'.

Havergate Island (near Orford) Marked thus on the Ordnance Survey map of 1805, and as simply *Havergate* on Hodskinson's map of 1783. Earlier spellings are needed, but possibly from Old English *hæfer* 'a he-goat' in view of nearby Gedgrave ('goats' grove').

Haverhill *Hauerhella*, *Haverhol* 1086 (Domesday Book), *Haverhell* 1158. Probably 'the hill where oats are grown', from Old English **hæfera* and *hyll*. Alternatively the first element may be Old English *hæfer* 'a he-goat', thus 'the hill where goats graze'. The local pronunciation is 'hayvrill'.

Hawkedon *Hauokeduna*, *Hauochenduna* 1086 (Domesday Book), *Hafkindun* 1195, *Hauekedon* 1242. Probably' the hill frequented by hawks', from Old English *hafoc* (genitive case plural *hafoca*) and *dūn*. However some early spellings suggest 'the hill of a man called *Hafoca', from an Old English personal name (genitive case *-an*) derived from the name of the bird.

Hawstead *Haldsteda* 1086 (Domesday Book), *Haldstede*, *Halstede* 12th century. 'The place of refuge or shelter (for livestock), the cattle farm', from Old English *h(e)ald* and *stede*. The local pronunciation is 'haw-st'd'. Halstead in Essex is identical in origin and meaning.

Hazelwood Common & Hall (near Aldeburgh) Marked *Hazelwood Hall* on the Ordnance Survey map of 1837, named from *Haselewod* 1254, *Haselwode* 1327, 'the hazel-tree wood', from Old English *hæsel* and *wudu*.

Helmingham *Helming(h)eham* 1086 (Domesday Book), *Helmingeham* 1173. 'The homestead of the family or followers of a man called Helm', from an Old English personal name with *-inga-* (genitive case of *-ingas* 'people of') and *hām*. Helmingham in Norfolk is identical in origin and meaning.

Hemingstone *Hamingestuna*, *Hemingestuna* 1086 (Domesday Book), *Hemingeston* 1212. 'The farmstead or estate of a man called Hemingr', from Old English *tūn* and an Old Scandinavian personal name. The local pronunciation is 'hemmings-t'n'.

Hemley *Helmelea*, *Halmeleia* 1086 (Domesday Book), *Helmele* 1219, 1327. 'The woodland clearing of a man called *Helma', from Old English *lēah* and an Old English personal name.

Hengrave *Hemegretham* 1086 (Domesday Book), *Hemegrede c.*1095. 'The grassy meadow of a man called Hemma', from an Old English personal name and **grēd* (the *-am* in the Domesday spelling is a Latin accusative case ending).

Henham (near Blythburgh) *Henham* 1086 (Domesday Book), 1207. 'The high (or chief) homestead or village', from Old English *hēah* (dative case *hēan*) and *hām*. Henham in Essex is identical in origin and meaning.

Henley *Henleia, Henle* 1086 (Domesday Book), *Henleye* 1242. 'The high (or chief) wood or woodland clearing', from Old English *hēah* (dative case *hēan*) and *lēah*.

Henstead *Henestede* 1086 (Domesday Book), *Henstede* 1254. Probably 'the place frequented by hens (of wild birds)', from Old English *henn* and *stede*.

Hepworth *Hepworda* 1086 (Domesday Book), *Hepewurde* 1193, *Hepwrthe* 1196. Possibly 'the enclosure or enclosed farmstead of a man called **Heppa*', from Old English *worth* and an Old English personal name. Alternatively, 'the enclosure where rosehips grow', from Old English *hēope*.

Herringfleet *Herlingaflet* 1086 (Domesday Book), *Herlingflet* 1254. 'The creek or stream of the family or followers of a man called **Herela*', from an Old English personal name with *-inga-* (genitive case of *-ingas* 'people of') and *flēot*. Now some four miles inland, Herringfleet was once on a broad estuary of the Rivers Waveney and Yare. The present form of the name is probably the result of popular etymology.

Herringswell *Hyrningwella, Herningawella* 1086 (Domesday Book), *Hyrningcwylle* 11th century. Possibly 'the spring or stream by the horn-shaped or curving hill', from Old English **hyrning* and *wella*.

Hessett *Heteseta* [*sic*, for *Hece-*] 1086 (Domesday Book), *Heggeset* 1225. 'The fold (for animals) with a hedge', from Old English *hecg* and *(ge)set*.

Heveningham *Heueniggeham* 1086 (Domesday Book), *Heveningham* 1200. 'The homestead of the family or followers of a man called **Hefīn*', from an Old English personal name with *-inga-* (genitive case of *-ingas* 'people of') and *hām*. The local pronunciation is 'hevning'm' or 'henning'm'.

Higham (near Barrow) *Heyham* 1275, *Hegham* 1303. Identical in origin and meaning with the following name.

Higham (near Stratford St Mary) *Hecham* 1042-66 (in a 12th century copy of an Anglo-Saxon charter), *Heihham* 1086 (Domesday Book). 'The high (or chief) homestead or village', from Old English *hēah* and *hām*. The local pronunciation is 'high'm'.

Hinderclay *Hild(e)ric(es)lea c.*1000 (in a 13th century copy of an Anglo-Saxon charter), *Hilderclea* 1086 (Domesday Book). 'The woodland clearing of a man called *Hildrīc', from Old English *lēah* and an Old English personal name. The local pronunciation is 'hin-der-clay'.

Hintlesham *Hintlesham* 1035-44 (in a 13th century copy of an Anglo-Saxon will), 1086 (Domesday Book), *Huntlesham* 1235. 'The homestead or village of a man called *Hyntel', from an Old English personal name and Old English *hām*. The local pronunciation is 'hint'l-sh'm'.

Hitcham *He(t)cham* 1086 (Domesday Book), *Heccham* 1198. 'The homestead or enclosure with a hedge or hatch-gate', from Old English *hecg* or *hecc* with either *hām* or *hamm*.

Holbrook *Holebroc* 1086 (Domesday Book), 1177. 'The hollow brook, the brook in a hollow', from Old English *hol* and *brōc*.

Hollesley *Holeslea* 1086 (Domesday Book), *Holesle* 1254. 'The wood or woodland clearing of the hollow', from Old English *hol* (genitive case *holes*) and *lēah*. The 'hollow' may refer to the small valley here or to the coastal feature of Hollesley Bay. The local pronunciation is 'hozelee'.

Holton (near Halesworth) *Holetuna* 1086 (Domesday Book), *Holeton* 1254. 'The farmstead or estate in or near a hollow, or of a man called *Hola', from Old English *tūn* and either Old English *hol* or an Old English personal name.

Holton St Mary *Holetuna* 1086 (Domesday Book), *Holeton* 1254. Identical in origin and meaning with the previous name. The distinguishing affix is from the dedication of the church.

Holwell Row (near Mildenhall) Marked thus on Hodskinson's map of 1783 and on the Ordnance Survey map of 1837, possibly 'the holy spring' from Old English *hālig* and *wella*, with Middle English *rowe* 'row of houses, hamlet'.

Homersfield *Humbresfelda* 1086 (Domesday Book), *Humbresfeld c*.1130. Probably 'the open land of a man called Hūnbeorht', from Old English *feld* and an Old English personal name. The man named is possibly to be identified with *Hūnbeorht*, bishop of Elmham (*c*.820-870). The local pronunciation is 'hummersfield'.

Honington *Hunegetuna* 1086 (Domesday Book), *Hunegeton* 1254. Probably 'the farmstead or estate of the family or followers of a man called Hūn(a)', from an Old English personal name with *-inga-* (genitive case of *-ingas* 'people of') and *tūn*.

Hoo Green *Ho* 1042-66 (in a 12th century copy of an Anglo-Saxon charter), *Hou*, *Hoi* 1086 (Domesday Book). '(The place at) the spur of land', from Old English *hōh* (dative case *hōe*).

Hopton (near Market Weston) *Hopetuna* 1086 (Domesday Book), *Hopeton* 12th century. 'The farmstead or estate in a small enclosed valley or enclosed plot of land', from Old English *hop* and *tūn*.

Hopton on Sea (historically in Suffolk, transferred to Norfolk in the boundary change of 1974) *Hoppetuna*, *Opituna* 1086 (Domesday Book), *Hopeton* 1242. Identical in origin and meaning with the previous name.

Horham *Horham c*.946 (in a 13th century copy of an Anglo-Saxon will), *Horam* 1086 (Domesday Book). 'The dirty or muddy homestead or enclosure', from Old English *horu* 'filth, dirt, mud' and either *hām* or *hamm*. The local pronunciation is 'horram'.

Horningsheath, *see* Horringer.

Horringer (a variant of Horningsheath, and now the usual form of the name) *Horning(g)esh'de*, *-hæth c*.946 (in a 13th century copy of an Anglo-Saxon will), *Horningeserda*, *Horningesworda* 1086 (Domesday Book), *Horningeseorthe* 11th century, *Horning(g)esherth Magna*, *-Parva* 1254. From Old English *horning* 'a horn-shaped feature, a bend' (probably referring to a bend in the River Linnet, or even an early name for the river itself in the sense 'winding stream'), to which has been added Old English *hǣth* 'heath', varying with Old English *worth* 'enclosure' and (principally) Old English *erth* 'ploughed land'. It is *Horningsherth* (alongside *Horringer Green & Hall*) on Hodskinson's map of 1783, and *Horningsheath or Horringer* on the Ordnance Survey map of 1837. The current spelling Horringer no doubt represents a worn-down spoken form of the name (*Hor(n)ingser(th)* > *Horingser* > *Horinger*), as against the more conservatively preserved written form Horningsheath. The local pronunciation is 'horrin-jer'.

Hoxne *Hoxne* c.946 (in a 13th century copy of an Anglo-Saxon will), *Hox(a)na*, *Hoxa* 1086 (Domesday Book). Probably from Old English *hōh-sinu* 'a heel sinew, a hock', here used figuratively with reference to a spur of land (probably the narrow east-west ridge on which the church stands) thought to resemble a horse's hock. The local pronunciation is 'hocks'n'.

Hulver Street (near Henstead) Marked as *Hulver Heath* on Hodskinson's map of 1783, from dialect *hulver* (Middle English *hulvere*) 'holly' and with *street* in the sense 'hamlet'.

Hundon *Hune(n)dana* 1086 (Domesday Book), *Huneden* 1219. 'The valley of a man called Hūna', from Old English *denu* and an Old English personal name (genitive case -*an*). The spelling with -*don* (as if from Old English *dūn* 'hill') is a later development.

Hundred River There are two Suffolk rivers with this name. One flows into the sea south of Kessingland, and is so called because it formed the boundary between the medieval Hundreds of Mutford and Blything. The other, flowing into the Meare at Thorpeness and marked *The Hundred River* on the Ordnance Survey map of 1837, formed the boundary between the medieval Hundreds of Blything and Plomesgate.

Hunston *Hunterstuna* 1086 (Domesday Book), *Hunterston* 1197. 'The farmstead or estate of the hunter or huntsman', from Old English **huntere* and *tūn*.

Huntingfield *Huntingafelde* 1086 (Domesday Book), *Huntingefeld* c.1180. 'The open land of the family or followers of a man called Hunta (the hunter or huntsman)', from an Old English personal name with *-inga-* (genitive case of *-ingas* 'people of') and *feld.*

Hussey Green (near Fressingfield) Marked thus on Hodskinson's map of 1783 and on the Ordnance Survey map of 1837, named from *Husseio* 12th century, *Hussegh* 1275. Etymology uncertain, but possibly 'the island (of dry or higher ground) where certain tendril-like plants grow', from Old English *hysse* and *ēg.*

Icklingham *Ecclingaham* 1086 (Domesday Book), *Ikelingeham* 1242. 'The homestead of the family or followers of a man called *Ycel', from an Old English personal name with *-inga-* (genitive case of *-ingas* 'people of') and *hām.* There was an important Romano-British settlement site here (near to where the Icknield Way crosses the River Lark), probably to be identified with *Camboritum* 'the crooked ford' recorded in the 4th century Antonine Itinerary.

Icknield Way (prehistoric trackway from Dorset to Norfolk, crossing the north west corner of Suffolk) Recorded as *Iccenhilde weg* and *Icenhylte* in 903 (in 10th and 12th century copies of Anglo-Saxon charters). These forms can be explained as 'the slope and the wood of a man called *Icca', from Old English *h(i)elde* and **hylte.* Alternatively, it is possible that there is some connection with the *Iceni*, the Iron Age tribe who once inhabited Norfolk and the northern half of Suffolk.

Ickworth *Ikewrth* c.946 (in a 13th century copy of an Anglo-Saxon will), *Iccawurthe* 1047-65 (in a 12th century copy of an Anglo-Saxon writ), *Kkewortham* [*sic*, for *Ickewortham*] 1086 (Domesday Book). 'The enclosure or enclosed farmstead of a man called *Icca', from Old English *worth* and an Old English personal name.

Iken *Icanho* late 9th century (Anglo-Saxon Chronicle in the annal for 654), *Ykene* 1212, *Ikano* 1254. 'The heel or spur of land of a man called *Ica', from Old English *hōh* and an Old English personal name (genitive case *-an*). The Chronicle entry for 654 records the establishment of a model monastery here by St Botolph (it was destroyed by Viking invaders in the winter of 869-70). The local pronunciation is 'ike'n'.

Ilketshall St Andrew, St Lawrence & St Margaret *Ilcheteleshala, Elcheteshala, Ulkesala* 1086 (Domesday Book), *Ilketeleshal* 1186, *Hulketeleshal* 1228. 'The detached unit of land of a man called *Ylfketill', from Old English *halh* and an Old Scandinavian personal name. The distinguishing affixes are from the dedications of the churches (on record from the late 12th century). In the early spellings, the mutated form *Ylfketill* of the personal name alternates with the standard variant *Ulfketill* (common in the Danelaw areas and in fact the name of the famous Ealdorman of East Anglia *c*.1004-16, Ulfketill or Ulfkell Snilling). The local pronunciation is 'ilka-shawl' or 'ilka-sh'l'.

Ingham *Ingham* 1086 (Domesday Book), *c*.1095, *Hingham* 12th century. Possibly 'the homestead or village of a man called Inga', from an Old English personal name and *hām*, although it has recently been suggested that the first element of this name, and of Ingham in Lincolnshire and Norfolk, may be a word meaning 'the Inguione', a member of the ancient Germanic tribe called the *Inguiones* mentioned by Tacitus and Pliny.

Instead Manor House (near Weybread) Named from *Is(e)stede c*.946 (in a 13th century copy of an Anglo-Saxon will), *Isteda* 1086 (Domesday Book), *Istede* 1463. Probably 'the pasture or homestead of a man called *Īsa', from Old English *stede* and an Old English personal name (genitive case *-an*). The spelling change of *I-* to *In-* is apparently a late development.

Ipswich *Gipes wic* 993 (Anglo-Saxon Chronicle), *Gipeswic, Gypeswiz, Gepeswiz* 1086 (Domesday Book), *Gipeswic, Gypeswic* 12th century (Anglo-Saxon Chronicle). Possibly 'the harbour or trading centre of a man called *Gip', from an Old English personal name and Old English *wīc*. Alternatively the first element may rather be an Old English *gip(s)*, *gypes* 'opening, gap' (with reference to the wide estuary of the River Orwell). In the early forms, the spelling *Gip-* represents a pronunciation 'Yip' with a 'soft' *G*: the current form *Ipswich* with loss of the initial consonant is first on record in the mid-13th century.

Ixworth *Gyxeweorde c*.1040 (Anglo-Saxon charter), *Giswortha, Icsewrda* 1086 (Domesday Book). 'The enclosure or enclosed farmstead of a man called *Gicsa or *Gycsa', from Old English *worth* and an Old English personal name.

Ixworth Thorpe *Torp* 1086 (Domesday Book), *Ixeworth thorp* 1305. 'The outlying farmstead or secondary settlement dependant on Ixworth', from Old Scandinavian *thorp, see* previous name.

62

Kedington *Kydington* 1043-5 (in a 13th century copy of an Anglo-Saxon will), *Kidituna* 1086 (Domesday Book), *Kedinton* 1200. Probably 'the farmstead or estate associated with a man called Cyda', from an Old English personal name with medial connective *-ing-* ('called after') and *tūn*. The local pronunciation is 'keddingt'n' or 'kett'n'.

Kelsale *Chylesheala, Keleshala* 1086 (Domesday Book), *Keleshale* 1254. 'The nook of land or hollow of a man called *Cēl(i) or Cēol', from Old English *halh* and an Old English personal name.

Kennet, River Recorded as *Kenet* in 1249, *see* Kentford.

Kentford *Cheneteforde* 11th century, *Keneteford* 1203. 'The ford over the River Kennet', from Old English *ford* and an ancient Celtic river-name (of uncertain meaning). The river (*Kenet* 1249) rises in Cambridgeshire and gives name to the village of Kennett in that county. The ford was where the river is crossed by the Icknield Way.

Kenton *Chenetuna, Kenetuna* 1086 (Domesday Book), *Kenetona* 1179. Probably 'the royal manor or estate', from Old English *cyne-* and *tūn*. Alternatively the first element may be the Old English male personal name *Cēna*.

Kentwell Hall (in Long Melford) Marked thus on Hodskinson's map of 1783, named from *Kanewella* 1086 (Domesday Book), *Kenetewell* 1168. Probably 'the stream called *Kenet*', from an ancient Celtic river-name (of uncertain meaning) with Old English *wella* 'spring, stream'. The river-name (identical with the Kennet that gives name to Kentford) could either refer to the small tributary of the River Glem rising to the north of the Hall, or be an early name for the River Glem itself.

Kersey *Cæresige* 1000-2 (in an 11th century copy of an Anglo-Saxon will), *Careseia* 1086 (Domesday Book), *Kerseye* 1235. 'The island (of higher ground) where cress grows', from Old English *cærse* and *ēg*. The *ēg* here refers to the promontory on which the church stands, and abundant watercress, formerly harvested commercially as a crop, is still found in the Kersey Brook (a tributary of the River Brett). **Kersey Tye** (marked thus on Hodskinson's map of 1783) contains dialect *tye* (from Old English *tēag*) 'a large common pasture'.

Kesgrave *Gressegraua* [*sic*] 1086 (Domesday Book), *Kersigrave* 1231, *Kerssegrave* 1254. Etymology uncertain: the second element could be Old English *grāf(a)* 'grove, coppiced wood' or *græf* 'pit, trench, ditch', the first element is probably Old English *cærse* 'cress'.

Kessingland *Kessingelanda* 1086 (Domesday Book), *Kessingeland* 1219. 'The cultivated land or estate of the family or followers of a man called *Cyssi', from an Old English personal name with *-inga-* (genitive case of *-ingas* 'people of') and *land*.

Kettlebaston *Kitelbeornastuna* 1086 (Domesday Book), *Ketelberneston* 1208. 'The farmstead or estate of a man called Ketilbiorn', from Old English *tūn* and an Old Scandinavian personal name.

Kettleburgh *Chetelberia, Ketelbiria* 1086 (Domesday Book), *Ketelberwe* 1235. Probably 'the hill or mound by the deep valley', from Old English *cetel* (with *K-* through Scandinavian influence) and *beorg*. The local pronunciation is 'ket'l-bruh'.

King's Fleet (a tributary of the River Deben near its mouth) Marked thus on Hodskinson's map of 1783, from *fleet* (Old English *flēot*) 'inlet, creek, stream'.

Kingston (near Woodbridge) *Kingestun* 1042-66 (in a 12th century copy of an Anglo-Saxon charter), *Kyngestuna* 1086 (Domesday Book). 'The king's estate, the royal manor', from Old English *cyning* and *tūn*. It may be significant that this place lies on the River Deben on the opposite bank to the Anglo-Saxon royal cemetery at Sutton Hoo. The local Kyson Hill & Point have a worn-down form of the same name.

Kirkley *Kirkelea* 1086 (Domesday Book), *Kirkele* 13th century. 'The woodland clearing by or belonging to a church', from Old Scandinavian *kirkja* (probably replacing Old English *cirice*) and Old English *lēah*.

Kirton *Kirketuna* 1086 (Domesday Book), *Kirketon* 1285. 'The manor or village with a church', from Old Scandinavian *kirkja* (probably replacing Old English *cirice*) and Old English *tūn*. Kirton in Lincolnshire is identical in origin and meaning.

Knettishall *Ghenetessala, Gnedeshalla* 1086 (Domesday Book), *Gnatteshale* 1188. Possibly 'the nook or hollow of the gnat' thus referring to gnat-infested land, from Old English *gnætt* and *halh*. However the noun *gnætt* may well be used as a personal name here, thus 'nook of land or hollow belonging to a man called Gnætt'. The local pronunciation is 'netti-shawl' or 'netti-sh'l'.

Knodishall *Chenotessala, Cnotesheala* 1086 (Domesday Book), *Knodeshal* 1234. Probably 'the nook of land or hollow of a man called *Cnott', from Old English *halh* and an Old English personal name. Alternatively the first element could be Old English **cnott* 'a hillock'. The local pronunciation is 'noddi-shawl' or 'noddi-sh'l'.

Lackford *Le(a)cforda* 1086 (Domesday Book), *Leacforde c*.1095. 'The ford where leeks grow', from Old English *lēac* and *ford*. The river-name **Lark** (first recorded as such in 1735) is a so-called back-formation from the place-name (although the expected form would have been *Lack*). The ford was where the river is crossed by the Icknield Way (a much earlier, Romano-British, name for the ford may have been *Camboritum*, *see* Icklingham).

Lake Lothing (the estuary of the River Waveney at Lowestoft) Marked thus on Hodskinson's map of 1783, so named from the medieval Hundred of Lothingland, which is recorded as *Luthinglond c*.946 (in a 13th century copy of an Anglo-Saxon will), *Ludingalanda* 1086 (Domesday Book), 'the land or district of a man called Hlūd or Luda', from an Old English personal name with *-inga-* (genitive case of *-ingas* 'people of') and *land*.

Lakenheath *Lacingahith* 1015-6 (in a 14th century copy of an Anglo-Saxon charter), *Lakinghethe* 1021-3 (in a 15th century copy of an Anglo-Saxon charter), *Lakingehethe* 1086 (Domesday Book). 'The landing-place of the people living by the stream(s), or of the family or followers of a man called Lāca', from Old English *lacu* or an Old English personal name with *-inga-* (genitive case of *-ingas* 'people of') and *hȳth*. Various feeders of the Little Ouse River flow nearby, and the inland harbour (*hȳth*) must have been significant at an early date: in 1086 (Domesday Book) there is mention of a fishing boat and fisheries. The local pronunciation is 'layk'nheath'.

Landguard Common & Point (near Felixstowe) Marked as *Langar Common* on Hodskinson's map of 1783, as *Langer Common & Point* on the Ordnance

Survey map of 1805, and of course the site of **Landguard Fort** (first built 1625) which is *Langar Fort* in 1783, *Langer or Landguard Fort* in 1805. An earlier spelling is *Langhere* 1294. 'The long promontory or point of land', from Old English *lang* and *gāra* 'a gore, a triangular piece of ground'. The present form of the name, clearly influenced by the function of the fort to 'guard the land', is the result of popular etymology.

Langham *Langham* 1086 (Domesday Book), *Langeham* 1205. 'The long homestead or village', from Old English *lang* and *hām*. Langham in Norfolk is identical in origin and meaning.

Langton Green (in Eye) Marked thus on the Ordnance Survey map of 1837, named from *Langeton* 1286, *Langton* 1316, 'the long farmstead or estate', from Old English *lang* and *tūn*.

Lark, River Recorded thus in 1735, and marked on Hodskinson's map of 1783 as *Larke*, a back-formation from Lackford. The change from the expected *Lack* to *Lark* may have been influenced by other Suffolk streams apparently named from birds (*see* Dove, Linnet and Wren). An earlier (11th century) description of the river as *Wridewellan* 'the winding stream' gave name to Wordwell and Worlington.

Lavenham *Lauanham* 962-91 (in an 11th century copy of an Anglo-Saxon will), *Lauenham* 1086 (Domesday Book), *Lavenham* 1254. 'The homestead of a man called Lāfa', from an Old English personal name (genitive case -*an*) and *hām*. The local pronunciation is 'lav'n'm'.

Lawshall *Lawessela* 1086 (Domesday Book), *Laweshell* 1194. 'The dwelling or shelter by a hill or mound', from Old English *hlāw* with either *sele* or **sell*. The local pronunciation is 'law-sh'l' or 'law-shaw'.

Laxfield *Laxefelda*, *Lessafeld* 1086 (Domesday Book), *Lexefelde* 1168. 'The open land of a man called *Leaxa', from Old English *feld* and an Old English personal name.

Layham *Hligham* 1000-2 (in an 11th century copy of an Anglo-Saxon will), *Leiham* 1086 (Domesday Book), *Laiham* 1207. 'The homestead with a shelter or refuge', from Old English **hlīg* and *hām*. The local pronunciation is 'lay'm'.

Leavenheath *heath of Levynhey* 1292, *Levenesheth* 1351. 'The heath at Levin's enclosure', from the Middle English personal name or surname *Levin* (Old English *Lēofwine*) and *hey* (Old English *gehæg*), with *hethe* (Old English *hǣth*). The local pronunciation is 'levv'nheath'.

Leiston *Leistuna*, *Leestuna* 1086 (Domesday Book), *Legestona* 1168. Probably 'the farmstead or estate with a beacon-fire', from Old English *līeg*, *lēg* (genitive case *-es*) and *tūn*. The local pronunciation is 'lay-st'n'.

Letheringham *Ledringaham*, *Letheringaham* 1086 (Domesday Book), *Letheringham* 1235. Probably 'the homestead of the family or followers of a man called Lēodhere', from an Old English personal name with *-inga-* (genitive case of *-ingas* 'people of') and *hām*.

Levington *Leuetuna*, *Leuentona* 1086 (Domesday Book), *Leuington* 1254. Probably 'the farmstead or estate of a man called Lēofa', from an Old English personal name (genitive case *-an*) and *tūn*.

Lidgate *Litgata* 1086 (Domesday Book), *Lidgate* 1254. '(The place at) the swing-gate', from Old English *hlid-geat*. The 'swing-gate' may have been one to prevent cattle (or other livestock) straying from pasture across a road or on to arable land. The local pronunciation is 'lid-gate' or 'lid-g't'.

Lindsey *Balesheia* [*sic*, for *Lalesheia*] 1086 (Domesday Book), *Lealeseia* c.1095, *Lelleseye* 1233, *Lelesseye* 1327. 'The island (of dry or higher ground) of a man called *Lelli*', from Old English *ēg* and an Old English personal name (genitive case **Lelles*). The *ēg* was probably the site of the 12th century motte-and-bailey castle here. The change from medial *-l-* to *-n-* (*Lel-* to *Len-*, *Lin-*) in this name seems to date from the late medieval period, and the intrusive *-d-* is an even later development. The local pronunciation is 'lin-zee'. **Lindsey Tye** (marked thus on Hodskinson's map of 1783) contains dialect *tye* (from Old English *tēag*) 'a large common pasture'.

Linnet, River Not on record until 1834, so no doubt a whimsical name from the bird on the analogy of the Lark, of which this stream is a tributary.

Linstead Magna & Parva *Linstede* 1086 (Domesday Book), *Magna Linstede*, *Parva Linstede* 1254. 'The place where flax is grown, or where maple-trees grow', from Old English *stede* with either *līn* or *hlyn*. The distinguishing affixes are Latin *magna* 'great' and *parva* 'little'.

Little Fakenham, *see* Fakenham.

Little Green (in Gislingham)   Marked thus on the Ordnance Survey map of 1837, from *green* 'village green, hamlet'.

Little London (near Wetherden)   Marked thus on Hodskinson's map of 1783 and on the Ordnance Survey map of 1837, an ironic or whimsical name, found also in other counties, for a small cluster of houses or a tiny hamlet. There are other instances of the name near Combs and in Eriswell.

Little Ouse River   Forming part of the boundary between north west Suffolk and Norfolk and recorded as *Owse parva* 1575, *Little Ouse* 1735, with the affix *little* (Latin *parva*) to distinguish it from the River Great Ouse (of which it is a tributary). Ouse is an ancient pre-English river-name, recorded in early sources as *Usan* (late 9th century, with Old English oblique case -*n*), *Use* (10th to 14th centuries), and is of uncertain meaning (probably simply 'water').

Little Stonham, *see* Stonham.

Livermere, Great   *Leuuremer* 1042-66 (in a 12th century copy of an Anglo-Saxon charter), *Liuermera* 1086 (Domesday Book), *Liuermere c.*1095. Probably 'the liver-shaped pool, or pool with thick muddy water', from Old English *lifer* and *mere*. However it is possible that the original first element was Old English *lǣfer* 'rush, reed, iris'. The affix *Great* distinguishes it from **Little Livermere**, recorded as *Litla Liuermera* in 1086 (Domesday Book).

Long Melford, *see* Melford.

Loudham Hall (near Pettistree)   Marked thus on the Ordnance Survey map of 1837, named from *Ludham, Ludeham* 1086 (Domesday Book), *Loudham* 1327. 'The homestead or village of a man called *Hlūda', from Old English *hām* and an Old English personal name.

Lound *Lunda* 1086 (Domesday Book), *Lund* 1254. 'The small wood or grove', from Old Scandinavian *lundr*. Lound in Lincolnshire is identical in origin and meaning.

Lowestoft *Lothu Wistoft* 1086 (Domesday Book), *Lothewistoft* 1212. 'The curtilage or homestead of a man called Hlothvér', from an Old Scandinavian personal name and Old Scandinavian *toft*. The local pronunciation is 'lowerstoft' or 'lowstoft' or 'lowstof'.

Market Weston, *see* Weston.

Marlesford *Marlesforda, Merlesforda* 1086 (Domesday Book), *Marlesford* 1235. Probably 'the ford of a man called *Mǣrel', from Old English *ford* and an Old English personal name. There is a crossing of a tributary of the River Alde here. The local pronunciation is 'marls-f'd'.

Martlesham *Merlesham* 1086 (Domesday Book), *Marlesham* 1216, *Martelsham* 1254. Etymology uncertain, but possibly 'the homestead or village of a man called *Mǣrel', from an Old English personal name (as in Marlesford) and Old English *hām*, then perhaps influenced at an early date by the Norman-French personal name *Martel* or by the following place-name. **Martlesham Creek** is marked thus on Hodskinson's map of 1783. The local pronunciation is 'martl-sh'm'.

Martley Hall (in Easton) Marked thus on Hodskinson's map of 1783 and on the Ordnance Survey map of 1837, named from *Martele, Martelaia, Mertlega* 1086 (Domesday Book), 'the woodland clearing frequented by martens', from Old English *mearth* and *lēah*.

Maypole Green (near Bradfield St George) Marked thus on the Ordnance Survey map of 1837 and as *May Pole Green* on Hodskinson's map of 1783, in allusion to a site where May festivities took place in earlier times. There is another Maypole Green near Dennington, marked thus on Hodskinson's map of 1783, and there is also a Maypole Green near Toft Monks in Norfolk.

Melford, Long *Melaforda* 1086 (Domesday Book), *Meleforde* c.1095. 'The ford by the mill', from Old English *myln* and *ford*, the later affix referring to the length of the village (the broad village street is over half a mile long). There is a crossing of a tributary of the River Stour here. The local pronunciation is 'melf'd' or 'melf't'.

Mellis *Melles, Mellels* 1086 (Domesday Book), *Melles* 1254. 'The mills', from Old English *myln* in a plural form (*-as*) and with South East dialect *-e-* for *-i/y-*.

Mells *Mealla* 1086 (Domesday Book), *Melnes* 12th century, *Melles* 1254. Like the previous name, from Old English *melnas* 'mills' (the South East dialect form of *myln* with plural *-as*).

Melton *Meltune* 1042-66 (in a 12th century copy of an Anglo-Saxon charter), *Meltuna* 1086 (Domesday Book). Possibly 'the farmstead or estate with a crucifix', from Old English *mǣl* and *tūn*. Alternatively the first element may be Old English *myln* (South East dialect *meln*) 'a mill' as in the previous names.

Mendham *Myndham*, *Mendham* c.946 (in a 13th century copy of an Anglo-Saxon will), *Mendham*, *Menneham* 1086 (Domesday Book). 'The homestead or village of a man called *Mynda', from Old English *hām* and an Old English personal name.

Mendlesham *Mundlesham*, *Menlessam* 1086 (Domesday Book), *Mendlesham* 1165. 'The homestead or village of a man called *Myndel', from Old English *hām* and an Old English personal name.

Metfield *Medefeld* 1214, 1229. 'The open land with meadow', from Old English *mǣd* and *feld*.

Mettingham *Metingaham* 1086 (Domesday Book), *Metingham* 1230. Probably 'the homestead of the family or followers of a man called *Metti', from an Old English personal name with *-inga-* (genitive case of *-ingas* 'people of') and *hām*. The local pronunciation is 'metting'm'.

Mickfield *Mucelfelda* 1086 (Domesday Book), *Miclefeld* c.1095. 'The large tract of open land', from Old English *micel* and *feld*.

Middleton *Mid(d)eltuna* 1086 (Domesday Book), *Midelton* 1203. 'The middle farmstead or estate', from Old English *middel* and *tūn*. Middleton in Norfolk is identical in origin and meaning.

Milden *Mellinga* [*sic*] 1086 (Domesday Book), *Meldinges* c.1130, *Melling* 1160, *Meldingg* 1254, *Milding* 1783. Etymology uncertain, but possibly '(the settlement of) the family or followers of a man called *Melda', from an Old English personal name and *-ingas*. Alternatively this may be 'the place where orach (milds) grows', from Old English *melde* with singular suffix *-ing*: the various kinds of this plant were widely used as fodder and in medicine in medieval times. The local pronunciation is 'mill-d'n'.

Mildenhall *Mildenhale* 1043-4 (in a 14th century copy of an Anglo-Saxon writ), *Mitdenehalla* [*sic*, for *Mildenehalla*] 1086 (Domesday Book), *Middelhala* 1130, *Mildehal* 1158. Probably 'the nook of land or hollow of a man called *Milda', from Old English *halh* with an Old English personal name (genitive case *-an*). Some early spellings show confusion with Old English *middel* 'middle'. The local pronunciation is 'mill-d'n-hawl'.

Mill River (a tributary of the River Deben), *see* Brightwell.

Minsmere Haven *Amynnesmere Havynne* 1452, named from the lost village of Minsmere, *Mensemara* 1086 (Domesday Book), 'the river-mouth lake', from Old Scandinavian *āmynni* 'the mouth of a river' and Old English *mere* 'a pool', later with Middle English *haven* 'a harbour'. The river-name **Minsmere** is a so-called back-formation from the place-name.

Monewden *Munegadena*, *Mungedena* 1086 (Domesday Book), *Munegeden* 1194. Probably 'the valley of the family or followers of a man called *Munda', from an Old English personal name with *-inga-* (genitive case of *-ingas* 'people of') and Old English *denu*. The local pronunciation is 'monna-d'n'.

Monks Eleigh, *see* Eleigh.

Monk Soham, *see* Soham.

Moulton *Muletuna* 1086 (Domesday Book), *Muleton* 1235. 'The farmstead or estate of a man called Mūla, or where mules are kept', from Old English *tūn* with either an Old English personal name or Old English *mūl* (genitive case plural *mūla*). Moulton St Michael in Norfolk is identical in origin and meaning.

Mutford *Mutford* 1086 (Domesday Book), 1212. Possibly 'the ford where meetings are held', from Old English *mōt* 'a moot, an assembly', and *ford*: the early spellings with *Mut-* instead of the expected *Mot-* are unusual but could reflect a dialect feature. In any case this place gave its name to a medieval Hundred, so it would probably have been the meeting-place of the Hundred.

Nacton *Nachetuna* 1086 (Domesday Book), *Naketun* 1233. Probably 'the farmstead or estate of a man called Hnaki', from Old English *tūn* and an Old Scandinavian personal name.

Naughton *Nawelton c.*1150, *Nauelton* 1191. Possibly 'the farmstead or estate of a man called Nagli', from Old English *tūn* and an Old Scandinavian personal name.

Nayland *Eilanda* 1086 (Domesday Book), *Neiland* 1227. '(The place at) the island (of dry or higher ground in a marshy area)', from Old English *ēg-land* with initial *N-* from Middle English *atten* 'at the'.

Nedging *Hnyddinge* 1000-2 (in an 11th century copy of an Anglo-Saxon will), *Neddinge* 1042-6 (in a 12th century copy of an Anglo-Saxon charter), *Niedinga* 1086 (Domesday Book), *Nedding* 1235. 'The place associated with a man called *Hnydda', from an Old English personal name with the singular suffix *-ing*. **Nedging Tye** (marked thus on Hodskinson's map of 1783) contains dialect *tye* (from Old English *tēag*) 'a large common pasture'.

Needham Market *Nedham* 13th century, *Nedham Markatt* 1388, *Nedeham Markett* 1511. 'The poor or needy homestead or village', from Old English *nēd* and *hām*, the later affix referring to the important early market (the right to have a market here was granted in 1226). The local pronunciation is 'need'm'. Needham in Norfolk is identical in origin and meaning, as is the next name.

Needham Street *Nedham c.*1185, 1219. Has the same origin as the previous name, with the later addition of *street* 'street of houses, hamlet'.

Nettlestead (near Somersham) *Nettlesteda* 1086 (Domesday Book), *Netlestede* 1139. 'The place where nettles grow', from Old English *netel(e)* and *stede*. Nettles may have been cultivated here as a crop for use as food or in medicine, or may suggest a deserted settlement site with enriched soil.

Newbourne *Neubrunna* 1086 (Domesday Book), *Neubrounia* 12th century, *Neubrunne* 1254. Usually explained as 'the new stream, i.e. perhaps one dry in summer', from Old English *nīwe* and *burna* (influenced by the cognate Old Scandinavian *brunnr*). However a recent suggestion that this is 'the nine springs', from Old Scandinavian *níu* and *brunnr*, is convincing: there are numerous springs in the vicinity.

Newmarket *Novum Forum* 1200, *Novum Mercatum* 1219, *la Newmarket* 1418. 'The new market town', from Middle English *newe* and *market* (rendered by Latin *novum*, *forum* and *mercatus* in the earliest forms). The right to have a market here was granted *c*.1200.

Newton (near Sudbury) *Niwetuna*, *Neuuetona* 1086 (Domesday Book). 'The new farmstead or settlement', from Old English *nīwe* and *tūn*.

Newton Hall (near Swilland) *Niuuetuna* 1086 (Domesday Book), *Neuweton* 1303. Identical in origin with the previous name.

Newton, Old *Newetuna*, *Newetona* 1086 (Domesday Book), *Neweton* 1196, *Eldneuton* 1418. Identical in origin with the previous names, with later affix Old English *(e)ald* 'old', *see* Gipping.

Norton *Nortuna*, *Nortune* 1086 (Domesday Book). 'The north farmstead or estate' (i.e. one lying to the north of another settlement, in this case perhaps Tostock), from Old English *north* and *tūn*. The same name is found in most English counties.

Nowton (near Sicklesmere) *Newetune* *c*.946 (in a 13th century copy of an Anglo-Saxon writ), *Neotuna* 1086 (Domesday Book), *Nouton* 1254. 'The new farmstead or settlement', from Old English *nēowe* (a variant of *nīwe*, *see* Newton) and *tūn*. The local pronunciation is 'noat'n'.

Oakley *Acle* 1086 (Domesday Book), *Akle* 1286. 'The wood or woodland clearing where oak-trees grow', from Old English *āc* and *lēah*.

Occold *Acholt* 1042-66 (in a 12th century copy of an Anglo-Saxon charter), *Acolt* 1086 (Domesday Book), *Achold* 1201. 'The oak-tree wood', from Old English *āc* and *holt*. The local pronunciation is 'ock'ld'.

Offton *Offetuna* 1086 (Domesday Book), *Offintone* 1166. 'The farmstead or estate of, or associated with, a man called Offa', from Old English *tūn* and an Old English personal name (genitive case *-an* in some early spellings alternating with medial *-ing-* 'associated with').

Old Newton, *see* Newton.

Onehouse *Anhus* 1052-66 (in a 13th century copy of an Anglo-Saxon will), *An(u)hus* 1086 (Domesday Book), *Onhus* 1275. 'The single or isolated house', from Old English *āna* and *hūs*. The local pronunciation is 'wunnuss'.

Ore, River Recorded as *Orus* (with Latin *-us*) 1577, *Ore* 1735, *see* Orford.

Orford *Oreford* 1164, 1212. 'The ford near the shore or the flat-topped ridge', from Old English *ōra* and *ford*. The reference here may be to a causeway across the marshes. **Orford Ness** (recorded thus on Hodskinson's map of 1783 and on the Ordnance Survey map of 1805) is from Middle English *ness* 'a headland'. The river-name **Ore** is a so-called back-formation from the place-name.

Orwell, River *Arewan* 11th century (Anglo-Saxon Chronicle), *Orewell* 1341, *the Vre* 1618. An ancient Celtic or pre-Celtic river-name *Arwe* (probably meaning 'swift one'), to which has been added Old English *wella* 'stream'. In Reyce's *Breviary* of 1618, it is said '*the Vre....drowneth it selfe in the bottomlesse well* in the mouth of the haven named of old from the said river *Vrewell haven*, butt in these dayes *Orewell haven*'.

Otley *Otelega, Oteleia* 1086 (Domesday Book), *Otteleia* 1198. 'The woodland clearing of a man called *Otta', from Old English *lēah* and an Old English personal name.

Oulton *Aleton* 1203, *Olton* 1220, *Alton* 1275, *Oulton* 1286. 'The farmstead or estate of a man called Áli', from Old English *tūn* and an Old Scandinavian personal name. **Oulton Broad** (marked thus on the Ordnance Survey map of 1837) contains *broad* in the sense 'extensive piece of water'.

Ousden *Uuesdana* 1086 (Domesday Book), *Uuesdene* 1198. Probably 'the valley of the owl', from Old English *ūf* (genitive case *ūfes*) and *denu*. The local pronunciation is 'ooz-d'n' or 'ows-d'n.

Pakefield *Paggefella* 1086 (Domesday Book), *Pagefeld* 1198, *Pakefeld* 1228. 'The open land of a man called Paga', from Old English *feld* and an Old English personal name.

Pakenham *Pakenham* c.946 (in a 13th century copy of an Anglo-Saxon will), *Pachenham* 1086 (Domesday Book). 'The homestead or village of a man called

*Pacca', from Old English *hām* and an Old English personal name (genitive case -*an*). The local pronunciation is 'payk-n'm'.

Palgrave *Palegrave* 962 (in a 13th century copy of an Anglo-Saxon charter), *Palegraue* c.1035 (in a 13th century copy of an Anglo-Saxon will), *Palegraua* 1086 (Domesday Book). Probably 'the grove where poles or stakes are got', from Old English *pāl* (genitive case plural *pāla*) and *grāf(a)*.

Pannington Hall (in Wherstead) Marked thus on the Ordnance Survey map of 1805, named from *Painetuna* 1086 (Domesday Book), *Pamton* 1242-3. Possibly 'the farmstead or estate of a man called Pǣgna', from an Old English personal name (genitive case -*an*, perhaps alternating with -*ing*- 'associated with') and *tūn*.

Parham *Perreham*, *Perham* 1086 (Domesday Book), *Pereham* 1206. Probably 'the homestead or enclosure where pear-trees grow', from Old English *peru* and either *hām* or *hamm*. The local pronunciation is 'parram'.

Peasenhall *Pese(n)hala*, *Pisehealle* 1086 (Domesday Book), *Pesenhal* 1228. 'The nook of land or hollow where peas grow', from Old English **pisen* and *halh*.

Peddars Way (long distance footpath following route of Roman road from Ixworth in Suffolk to Holme-next-the-Sea in Norfolk) Marked thus (also as *Peddars Road*) on the Ordnance Survey map of 1824, from Middle English *peddere* 'a pedlar'.

Pettaugh *Pet(t)ehaga* 1086 (Domesday Book), *Pethaghe* 13th century. Probably 'the hedged enclosure of a man called Pēota', from Old English *haga* and an Old English personal name. The local pronunciation is 'petta'.

Pettistree *Peterestrie* 1202, *Petrestre* 1253. Probably 'the tree of a man called Peter', from the Saint's name *Peter* and Middle English *tre* (Old English *trēow*).

Peyton Hall (in Ramsholt) Marked thus on Hodskinson's map of 1783 and on the Ordnance Survey map of 1805, named from *Peituna* 1086 (Domesday Book), *Peytone* 1327, 'the farmstead or estate of a man called Pǣga', from an Old English personal name and *tūn*.

Pin Mill (in Chelmondiston) Marked thus on Hodskinson's map of 1783 and on the Ordnance Survey map of 1805, perhaps so called with reference to the structure of the original mill that gave the present hamlet its name, 'the mill constructed using wooden pegs or pins', from Old English *pinn*.

Playford *Playford c.*1040 (in a 13th century copy of an Anglo-Saxon charter), *Plegeforda* 1086 (Domesday Book), *Pleiforda* 1130. 'The ford where play or sport takes place', from Old English *plega* and *ford*. There is a crossing of the River Fynn here.

Polstead *Polstede c.*962-91, 1000-2 (in 11th century copies of Anglo-Saxon wills), *Polesteda* 1086 (Domesday Book). 'The pool place', from Old English *pōl* and *stede*. A noteworthy feature of the 1000-2 document is that it contains a description of the bounds of Polstead and Withermarsh at that date.

Poslingford *Poslingeorda*, *Poslingewrda* 1086 (Domesday Book), *Poselingwrtha* 1195. 'The enclosure of the family or followers of a man called *Possel', from an Old English personal name with *-inga-* (genitive case of *-ingas* 'people of') and *worth*. The substitution of *ford* for the final element is only relatively recent (from the 17th century).

Poystreet Green (near Rattlesden) Marked as *Poy Street Green* on Hodskinson's map of 1783 and as *Poy Street or Posford Green* on the Ordnance Survey map of 1837, first element uncertain, possibly a surname, but it is to be noted that a small stream is crossed by a Roman road here (to which *street* may refer).

Preston St Mary *Preston* 1052-66 (in a 13th century copy of an Anglo-Saxon will), *Prestetona*, *Prestetune* 1086 (Domesday Book). 'The farmstead or estate of the priests', from Old English *prēost* (genitive case plural *prēosta*) and *tūn*. The affix is from the dedication of the church.

Purdis Farm (in Foxhall) Marked as *Purdis* on Hodskinson's map of 1783, and as *Purdeis Farm* on the Ordnance Survey map of 1805, earlier *Purdeys* or *Purdyes* 1561, so named from a family called *Purde(y)* who had lands in this area from the late 13th century.

Ramsholt *Ramesholt* 1086 (Domesday Book), 1166, *Ramisholt* 1291. Probably 'the wood or thicket where wild garlic grows', from Old English *hramsa* and *holt*. The local pronunciation is 'ram-solt'.

Rat, River (a tributary of the River Gipping), *see* Rattlesden.

Rattlesden *Rattesdene* 1042-66 (in a 12th century copy of an Anglo-Saxon charter), *Ratlesdena, Ratesdana* 1086 (Domesday Book), *Retlesden* 1198. Etymology uncertain, but possibly 'the valley of a man called *Rætel', from Old English *denu* and an Old English personal name. Alternatively the first element may be an Old English plant-name *hratele* (cf. ModE *rattle*). The river-name **Rat** (also known as Rattlesden River) is a so-called back-formation from the place-name.

Raydon *Reindune, Rienduna* 1086 (Domesday Book), *Reindun* c.1200. 'The hill where rye is grown', from Old English *rygen* (adjective) 'growing with rye' and *dūn*. This name is thus identical in origin and meaning with Reydon.

Rede *Reoda, Reda, Riete* 1086 (Domesday Book), *Rede* 1254. Etymology uncertain, possibly '(the place at) the clearing', from Old English *rēod*, rather than '(the place by) the reed-bed', from Old English *hrēod*, since there is high ground here. The local pronunciation is 'reed'.

Redgrave *Redgrafe* 11th century, *Redegraue* 1179. Possibly 'the pit or ditch where reeds grow', from Old English *hrēod* and *græf*. Alternatively, this may be 'the red grove', from Old English *rēad* and *grāf(a)*.

Redisham *Redesham* 1086 (Domesday Book), *Redisham* 1291. Probably 'the homestead or village of a man called *Rēad', from Old English *hām* and an Old English personal name.

Redlingfield *Radinghefelda* [*sic*] 1086 (Domesday Book), *Radlingefeld* 1166. 'The open land of the family or followers of a man called Rǣdel or *Rǣdla', from an Old English personal name with *-inga-* (genitive case of *-ingas* 'people of') and *feld*.

Rendham *Rimdham, Rindham* 1086 (Domesday Book), *Rindham* 1203. Possibly 'the cleared homestead', from Old English *hām* and the Old English adjective *rȳmed*. Alternatively, the first element may be an Old English *rind(e)* 'hill, edge, border'.

Rendlesham *Rendlæsham c.*731 (Bede's Ecclesiastical History of the English People, Latin version), *Rendlesham* c.890 (Bede, Old English version), 1086 (Domesday Book). Possibly 'the homestead or village of a man called *Rendel', from Old English *hām* and an Old English personal name. This interpretation follows that of Bede who describes Rendlesham as *uicus regius* 'a royal estate' and translates it as *mansio Rendili* 'the residence of Rendil'. However Bede may have been reinterpreting an older name, with the first element an Old English word **rendel* 'a border, edge or strip of land'. Whatever the origin of the name, the former existence of a royal hall here (that of the *Wuffingas*, the dynasty whose cemetery was at Sutton Hoo) has been confirmed by recent archaeology. The local pronunciation is 'rend'l-sh'm'.

Reydon *Rienduna* 1086 (Domesday Book), *Reydone* 1254. 'The hill where rye is grown', from Old English *rygen* (adjective) 'growing with rye' and *dūn*. The local pronunciation is 'ray-d'n'. Raydon has the same origin and meaning.

Rickinghall Inferior & Superior *Rikinghale c.*1000 (in a 13th century copy of an Anglo-Saxon charter), *Rikingahala, Richingehalla* 1086 (Domesday Book). 'The nook of land or hollow of the family or followers of a man called *Rīca', from an Old English personal name with *-inga-* (genitive case of *-ingas* 'people of') and *halh*. The distinguishing affixes are Latin *inferior* 'lower, nether' and *superior* 'higher, upper'.

Ringsfield *Ringesfelda, Ringesfella* 1086 (Domesday Book), *Ringefeld* 1235. Possibly 'the open land of a man called *Hring', from Old English *feld* and an Old English personal name. Alternatively, the first element may rather be the Old English word *hring* 'a ring' with reference to some lost circular feature (such as a henge monument or an enclosure).

Ringshall *Ringhesehla, Ringeshala* 1086 (Domesday Book), *Ringeshale* 1198. Etymology uncertain. Possibly 'the nook of land or hollow of a man called *Hring, or near a circular feature', from Old English *halh* with either an Old English personal name or Old English *hring* (*see* Ringsfield). Alternatively, perhaps 'the circular shelter (for animals)', from Old English *hring* and **(ge)sell*. The local pronunciation is 'ring-sh'l' or 'rinks'l'. In **Ringshall Stocks** (recorded thus on the Ordnance Survey map of 1837) the addition is from the word *stock* 'a tree-stump'.

Risby *Risebi, Riseby, Resebi* 1086 (Domesday Book), *Rissebi* 1166. 'The farmstead or village among the brushwood', from Old Scandinavian *hrís* and *bý*. Risby in Lincolnshire is identical in origin and meaning.

Rishangles *Risangra* 1086 (Domesday Book), *Rishangr* 1171. 'The wooded slope where brushwood grows', from Old English *hrīs* and *hangra*. Spellings resembling the modern form of the name appear from the mid-13th century, as in *Rissangeles* 1254. The local pronunciation is 'rish-ang'ls'.

Rotten End (near Peasenhall) Marked thus on Hodskinson's map of 1783, a somewhat derogatory name-type usually associated with soft boggy land (as probably in the name Rotten Row in London's Hyde Park), with *end* 'a district of a parish, a hamlet'.

Rougham Green *Rucham* c.946 (in a 13th century copy of an Anglo-Saxon will), c.1000 (in a 13th century copy of an Anglo-Saxon charter), *Ruhham* 1086 (Domesday Book). Probably 'the homestead or village on rough ground', from Old English *rūh* (adjective 'rough', here used as a noun) and *hām*. The local pronunciation is 'ruff'm'. Rougham in Norfolk is identical in origin and meaning.

Rumburgh *Romburch* c.1050, *Romburc, Ramburc* [sic] (Domesday Book), *Rumburg* c.1130. 'The wide stronghold, or the stronghold built of tree-trunks', from Old English *burh* and either Old English *rūm* 'wide' or **hruna* 'tree-trunk'. The local pronunciation is 'rumbruh'.

Rushbrooke *Ryssebroc* c.946-51 (in a 13th century copy of an Anglo-Saxon will), *Ryscebroc* 1086 (Domesday Book). 'The brook where rushes grow', from Old English **rysc* and *brōc*.

Rushmere *Riscemara, Ryscemara* 1086 (Domesday Book), *Russhemere* 1286. 'The pool where rushes grow', from Old English **rysc* and *mere*.

Rushmere St Andrew *Riscemara, Ryscemara* 1086 (Domesday Book), *Russemere* 1193-5. Identical in origin with the previous name. The distinguishing affix is from the dedication of the church.

St Cross South Elmham, *see* Elmham.

St Edmundsbury (district), a modern adoption of an early name of Bury St Edmunds, also preserved in the diocese-name of St Edmundsbury & Ipswich.

St James South Elmham, *see* Elmham.

St Margaret South Elmham, *see* Elmham.

St Michael South Elmham, *see* Elmham.

Sandlings, The (region of south east Suffolk characterized by its sandy soils) Referred to as *Sandling* in 1797, and as *The Sandlings* from the mid-19th century, earlier *Sandlands* 1735, from *sand* and *land* in the sense 'district'.

Santon Downham, *see* Downham.

Sapiston *Sapestuna* 1086 (Domesday Book), *Sapeston* 1204. From Old English *tūn* 'farmstead, estate, settlement' with an uncertain first element, possibly an Old English personal name or other as yet unidentified word.

Saxham, Great & Little *Saxham, Sexham* 1086 (Domesday Book), *Saxham Magna, Saxham Parva* 1254. Probably 'the homestead or village of the Saxons', from Old English *Seaxe* and *hām*. The early distinguishing affixes are Latin *magna* 'great' and *parva* 'little'.

Saxmundham *Saxmondeham, Sasmunde(s)ham* 1086 (Domesday Book), *Saxmundham* 1213. 'The homestead or village of a man called *Seaxmund', from Old English *hām* and an Old English personal name. The local pronunciation is 'sax-mund'm' (with the stress on the second syllable).

Saxtead *Saxteda* 1086 (Domesday Book), *Saxstede* 1202. Probably 'the place of a man called Seaxa', from Old English *stede* and an Old English personal name. **Saxtead Green** is marked as *Saxstead Green* on Hodskinson's map of 1783.

Seckford Hall (near Woodbridge) Marked thus on the Ordnance Survey map of 1805, named from *Sekeforda* 1086 (Domesday Book), *Secheford* 1206, 'the ford of a man called Secca', from an Old English personal name and *ford*. There is a crossing of an arm of the River Fynn near here.

Semer *Seamera* 1086 (Domesday Book), *Semere c.*1095. 'The lake pool', from Old English *sæ* and *mere*. The local pronunciation is 'see-mer'.

Shadingfield *Scadenefella* 1086 (Domesday Book), *Schadenesfeld* 1190. Probably 'the open land by the boundary valley', from Old English *scēad* and *denu* with *feld*. The reference is to the boundary of a medieval Hundred. The local pronunciation is 'shaddingfield'.

Shelland (near Rattlesden) *Sellanda* 1086 (Domesday Book), *Shevelond* 1234. 'The cultivated land on a shelf of level ground', from Old English *scelf* and *land*. The local pronunciation is 'shell'n'd'.

Shelley (near Raydon) *Scelfleage* 1000-2 (in an 11th century copy of an Anglo-Saxon will), *Sceueleia* [*sic*] 1086 (Domesday Book), *Schelfleye* 1254. 'The woodland clearing on a shelf or ledge', from Old English *scelf* and *lēah*.

Shimpling *Simplinga* 1086 (Domesday Book), *Simplengges* 1230, *Simpling* 1236, *Chimplingge* 1327. Probably '(the settlement of) the family or followers of a man called *Scimpel*, from an Old English personal name with the suffix *-ingas* 'people of'. Shimpling in Norfolk is identical in origin and meaning.

Shingle Street (on the coast near Hollesley) Marked thus on Hodskinson's map of 1783, from early Modern English *shingle* 'pebbles' and *street* 'hamlet'.

Shipmeadow *Scipmedu* 1086 (Domesday Book), *Shipmedwe* 1254. 'The meadow for sheep', from Old English *scēap* and *mǣd* (dative case *mǣdwe*).

Shotley *Scoteleia* 1086 (Domesday Book), *Schottele* 1242. Probably 'the woodland clearing on the steep slope', from Old English *sceōt* and *lēah*. Alternatively the first element could formally be Old English *sceot* 'shooting' or *sceote* 'a pigeon'.

Shottisham *Scotesham* 1086 (Domesday Book), *Schatesham* 1254, *Shettisham* 1313. Probably 'the homestead or village of a man called *Sceōt*, from Old English *hām* and an Old English personal name.

Sibton *Sib(b)etuna* 1086 (Domesday Book), *Sibbetun* 1156. 'The farmstead or estate of a man called Sibba', from Old English *tūn* and an Old English personal name.

Sicklesmere Marked thus on the Ordnance Survey map of 1836 and as *Sicklemere* on Hodskinson's map of 1783, probably from Old English *sīcel* 'a small stream' and *mere* 'a pool or pond'. The place lies on the River Lark.

Silverley's Green (near Cratfield) Marked as *Silverlace Green* on Hodskinson's map of 1783, and as *Silverleys Green* on the Ordnance Survey map of 1837, possibly from a surname *Silverley* (itself from either one of places called Silverley in Cambridgeshire or Silver Ley in Essex), with *green* 'village green, hamlet'.

Sizewell *Syreswell* 1240, *Syswell* 1280. Probably 'the spring or stream of a man called Sigehere', from an Old English personal name and Old English *wella*.

Snape *Snapes* 1086 (Domesday Book), *Snape* 1275. From Old English **snæp* 'boggy pasture' or the cognate Old Scandinavian *snap* 'poor pasture'. Snape in North Yorkshire is identical in origin and meaning.

Soham, Earl & Monk *Saham* 1086 (Domesday Book), *Earl Saham*, *Monks Saham* 1235. 'The homestead or village with a pool', from Old English **sā* and *hām*. The name refers to a large reedy lake (once stocked with fish) the site of which lay just to the west of Earl Soham village. Distinguishing affixes from early possession by the Earl of Norfolk and the monks of Bury St Edmunds.

Somerleyton *Sumerledetuna* 1086 (Domesday Book), *Sumerletun* c.1185. 'The farmstead or estate of a man called Sumarlithi', from Old English *tūn* and an Old Scandinavian personal name (a byname meaning 'summer traveller' found also in Somerton and denoting a warrior who went in summer on Viking expeditions). The local pronunciation is 'summer-layt'n' (with the stress on the third syllable).

Somersham *Sumersham* 1086 (Domesday Book), *Sumeresham* 1242. 'The homestead or village of a man called *Sumor', from Old English *hām* and an Old English personal name. The local pronunciation is 'summer-sh'm'.

Somerton *Sumerledetune* 1042-53, *Somerledetone* 1052-66 (in 13th century copies of Anglo-Saxon wills), *Sumerledetuna* 1086 (Domesday Book). Identical in origin and meaning with Somerleyton. The two earliest spellings may belong here or to Somerleyton. The local pronunciation is 'summer-t'n'.

Sotherton (near Westhall) *Sudretuna* 1086 (Domesday Book), *Sutherton* 1229. 'The southern farmstead or estate', from Old English *sūtherra* and *tūn*. The local pronunciation is 'suther-t'n'.

Sotterley *Soterlega* 1086 (Domesday Book), *Soterle* 1242. From Old English *lēah* 'a wood, a woodland clearing' with an uncertain first element, possibly an Old English personal name or other as yet unidentified word.

Southolt *Sudholda* 1086 (Domesday Book), *Sutholt* 1252. 'The southern wood', from Old English *sūth* and *holt*.

Southwold *Sudwolda* 1086 (Domesday Book), *Sudwald* 1227. 'The south woodland or forest', from Old English *sūth* and *wald*.

Spexhall *Specteshale* 1197, *Spicteshale* 1198. 'The nook of land or hollow frequented by the green woodpecker', from Old English **speoht* and *halh*. It is possible that the word **speoht* is used here as a personal name.

Sproughton *Sproeston* 1191, *Sprouton* 1198. 'The farmstead or estate of a man called Sprow', from Old English *tūn* and an Old English personal name. The local pronunciation is 'sprawt'n'.

Stanningfield *Stanfelda* 1086 (Domesday Book), *Stanefeld* 1197. 'The stony open land', from Old English *stān* 'stone' (alternating with the adjectival form **stānen* 'stony') and *feld*. Here the spelling *-ing-* is a later analogical development of the adjectival *-en*.

Stansfield *Stanesfelda*, *Stenesfelda* 1086 (Domesday Book), *Stanesfelde* c.1095. Probably 'the open land of a man called **Stān*', from Old English *feld* and an Old English personal name. Alternatively perhaps 'the open land of the stone', from Old English *stān* with reference to a standing stone or stony ground.

Stanstead *Stanesteda* 1086 (Domesday Book), *Stanstede* 1197. 'The stony place', from Old English *stān* 'stone' and *stede*. Stansted in Essex and Kent are identical in origin and meaning.

Stanton *Stantuna* 1086 (Domesday Book), *Stantun* 11th century. 'The farmstead or estate on stony ground', from Old English *stān* 'stone' and *tūn*. The same name is found in several other English counties. The affix in **Stanton Chare** (marked as *Stanton Char* on Hodskinson's map of 1783) is recorded as a surname *del* ('of the') *Charr* in 1283, from Old English **cearr* 'a turn, a bend', perhaps with reference to the marked bend in the Bury Road here: note too that there is a Roman villa-site at Stanton Chare, near to where Peddars Way was once joined by a Roman road.

Staverton Park (near Butley) Marked thus on the Ordnance Survey map of 1838, named from *Stauertuna, Stauretona* 1086 (Domesday Book), *Stauerton* 1190. 'The farmstead where stakes are made or obtained', from Old English **stæfer* and *tūn*. There is ancient woodland here.

Sternfield *Sternesfelda, Sterne(s)fella* 1086 (Domesday Book), *Sternefeld* 1235. Possibly 'the open land of a man called *Sterni', from Old English *feld* and an Old English personal name.

Stoke (in Ipswich) *Stoc* 970 (Anglo-Saxon charter), *Stoches* 1086 (Domesday Book), *Stoke* 1327, *St Mary Stoke* 1437. From Old English *stoc* 'an outlying farmstead, a secondary settlement'. It lies on the south bank of the River Orwell, across the river from the old town of Ipswich.

Stoke Ash *Stoca* mid-11th century, *Stoches* 1086 (Domesday Book), *Stokeaysche* 1524. From Old English *stoc* as in the previous name, with later addition from Middle English *a(i)sh* (Old English *æsc*) 'ash-tree'.

Stoke by Clare *Stoches* 1086 (Domesday Book), *Stokes near Clare* 1287. From Old English *stoc* as in the previous names, with addition from its proximity to Clare.

Stoke-by-Nayland *Stoke* c.946-c.951 (in a 13th century copy of an Anglo-Saxon will), 962-91 (in an 11th century copy of an Anglo-Saxon will), *Stokes* 1086 (Domesday Book), *Stokeneylond* 1272. From Old English *stoc* 'an outlying farmstead, a secondary settlement', with later addition from its proximity to Nayland.

Stonham Aspal, Earl Stonham & Little Stonham *Stonham* 1035-44 (in a 13th century copy of an Anglo-Saxon will), *Stanham* 1086 (Domesday Book), *Parva Stonham* 1219, *Stanham Comitis* 1254, *Aspalestonham* 1404. 'The homestead or village on stony ground', from Old English *stān* and *hām*. The distinguishing affixes *Aspal* and *Earl* are manorial, from the *de Aspale* family (from Aspall near Debenham) and *Earl* Roger Bigod, here in the 13th century. The early affixes are Latin *parva* 'little' and *comitis* 'of the earl'. The local pronunciation is 'stonn'm'.

Stour, River Recorded as *Sture* in 894 (Asser's *Life of King Alfred*) and other early sources. An ancient river-name, either Celtic or OE in origin, probably meaning 'the strong one'. This great river forms the ancient boundary between the East Saxons of Essex and the East Angles of Suffolk. There are no less than five major rivers in England with this name.

Stoven *Stouone* 1086 (Domesday Book), *Stovene* 1201. '(The place at) the tree-stump(s)', from either Old English or Old Scandinavian *stofn*. The local pronunciation is 'stuvv'n'.

Stow, West *Stowa* 1086 (Domesday Book), *Westowe* 1254. From Old English *stōw* 'place of assembly or holy place', later with the affix *west* to distinguish it from the other places called Stow. A significant Anglo-Saxon settlement dating from the 5th and 6th centuries has been discovered here.

Stowlangtoft *Stou, Stoua* 1086 (Domesday Book), *Stowelangetot* 13th century. From Old English *stōw* as in previous name, later with manorial affix from the *de Langetot* family, here in the early 13th century. The family took their name from Languetot in Normandy.

Stowmarket *Stou* 1086 (Domesday Book), *Stoumarket* late 12th century, *Stowmarket* 1268. From Old English *stōw* as in the previous names, the later addition referring to the important early market here (recorded in Domesday Book and as *forum de la Stowe* in 1253). The place gave its name to the medieval hundred of Stow, the meeting place of which would have been here. The original name of the settlement here seems to have been *Thorney*, *see* Thorney Green.

Stowupland *Stow Uplande* 1524. 'The higher land at Stow(market)', from Middle English *uplande*.

Stradbroke *Statebroc, Stetebroc* [*sic*, ? for *Stratebroc, Stretebroc*] 1086 (Domesday Book), *Stradebroc* 1168. Etymology uncertain, possibly 'the brook by a paved road', from Old English *strǣt* and *brōc*, but post-Domesday Book spellings suggest the first element may be Old English *strǣde* 'a pace, a stride', thus 'the brook that can be crossed in a stride'. The E-W road through the village crosses a small stream near Street Farm. The local pronunciation is 'stradbrook'.

Stradishall *Stratesella* 1086 (Domesday Book), *Strateshell* 1203, *Stradesele* 1327. 'The shelter (for animals) by a paved road', from Old English *strǣt* and **(ge)sell*. The local pronunciation is 'straddi-shawl'.

Stratford St Andrew *Straffort* 1086 (Domesday Book), *Strafford* 1254. 'The ford on the paved road', from Old English *strǣt* and *ford*, with later affix from the dedication of the church. There is a crossing of the River Alde here.

Stratford St Mary *Strætford, Stredford* 962-91 (in an 11th century copy of an Anglo-Saxon will), *Strætford* 975-1016 (Anglo-Saxon will), *Stratfort* 1086 (Domesday Book). Identical in origin with the previous name, but here 'the ford on the Roman road', referring to the important crossing of the River Stour by the Roman road from Colchester to Baylham: in fact Stratford has been identified with the Roman place-name *Ad Ansam* 'at the loop or river-bend' recorded in the 4th century Antonine Itinerary. The distinguishing affix is from the church dedication.

Stratton Hall (near Levington) *Strattuna* 1086 (Domesday Book), *Strattone* 1254. 'The farmstead or estate by the paved (or Roman) road', from Old English *strǣt* and *tūn*.

Stuston *Stutestuna* 1086 (Domesday Book), *Stuteston* c.1195, *Stuston* 1254. Probably 'the farmstead or estate of a man called *Stūt', from Old English *tūn* and an Old English personal name (no doubt a nickname from Old English *stūt* 'a gnat').

Stutton *Stuttuna, Stottuna* 1086 (Domesday Book), *Stutton* 1220. Probably 'the farmstead or estate on or by a stumpy hillock', from Old English **stūt* and *tūn*.

Sudbourne *Sutborne* 1042-66 (in a 12th century copy of an Anglo-Saxon charter), *Sutburna*, *Sutburne* 1086 (Domesday Book). 'The southern stream', from Old English *sūth* and *burna*.

Sudbury *Suthbyrig* 1000-2 (in an 11th century copy of an Anglo-Saxon will), *Sutberia* 1086 (Domesday Book). 'The southern fortified town or manor', from Old English *sūth* and *burh* (dative case *byrig*), so named in relation to Bury St Edmunds. The local pronunciation is 'sud-b'ree'.

SUFFOLK *Suffolke* 1043-5 (in a 13th century copy of an Anglo-Saxon will), *Suthfolce* 1047-65 (in a 12th century copy of an Anglo-Saxon writ), *Suthfolc*, *Suthfulc*, *Sudfolc* 1086 (Domesday Book). '(The territory of) the southern people (of the East Angles)', from Old English *sūth* and *folc*. It contrasts of course with Norfolk, 'the northern people' from Old English *north* and *folc*, recorded as *Norfolke* 1043-5 (in a 13th century copy of an Anglo-Saxon will), *Nordfolc* 1086 (Domesday Book), *Northfolce* late 11th century.

Sutton *Suthtuna* 1086 (Domesday Book), *Sutton* 1166. 'The southern farmstead or estate', from Old English *sūth* and *tūn*, so named in relation to Woodbridge.

Sutton Hoo *Hou*, *Hoi* 1086 (Domesday Book), *Hoo* 1442. From Old English *hōh* 'spur of land, hill-spur', with later addition from its proximity to Sutton. The remarkable Anglo-Saxon royal cemetery discovered here includes the famous ship burial of Rædwald, king of the East Angles (died 624/5).

Swefling *Sueflinga*, *Suestlingan* [*sic*, for *Sueft-*] 1086 (Domesday Book), *Sueftlinges* c.1150, *Swiftling* 1222. Probably '(the settlement of) the family or followers of a man called *Swiftel* or *Swæftel*', from an Old English personal name with the suffix *-ingas* 'people of'.

Swilland *Suinlanda* 1086 (Domesday Book), *Suinelanda* 1185. 'The tract of land where pigs are kept, the swine pasture', from Old English *swīn* and *land*.

Syleham *Silham* c.946 (in a 13th century copy of an Anglo-Saxon will), *Seilam*, *Seilanda* 1086 (Domesday Book), *Sileham* 1174. Probably 'the homestead or village at the boggy or miry place', from Old English *syle* or *sylu* and *hām* (alternating with *land* 'estate' in the second Domesday Book form). The church here stands in marshy ground by the River Waveney and is only accessible by a quarter-mile long causeway. The local pronunciation is 'sigh-l'm'.

Tangham Farm (in Capel St Andrew)   Marked as *Tangham House* on Hodskinson's map of 1783 and on the Ordnance Survey map of 1805, named from *Tangham* 1275, 'the homestead or enclosure on a spit of land', from Old English *tang* with either Old English *hām* or *hamm*. The name of the stream called **The Tang** (a tributary of Butley River) is no doubt a so-called back-formation from the place-name.

Tannington   *Tatintuna* 1086 (Domesday Book), *Tatingtone* 1254. 'The farmstead or estate associated with a man called Tāta', from an Old English personal name with medial connective *-ing-* ('called after') and *tūn*. The change from *Tat-* to *Tan-* is relatively late, as in *Tanyngton* 1524.

Tattingstone   *Tatistuna* [*sic*] 1086 (Domesday Book), *Tatingeston* 1219. Possibly 'the farmstead or estate of a man called *Tāting*', from Old English *tūn* and an Old English personal name. Alternatively 'the farmstead at the place belonging to a man called Tāta', from a different personal name with Old English suffix *-ing* and *tūn*.

Theberton   *Thewardetuna* [*sic*] 1086 (Domesday Book), *Tiberton* 1176, *Teberton* 1200. 'The farmstead or estate of a man called Thēodbeorht', from Old English *tūn* and an Old English personal name.

Thelnetham   *Theluetteham*, *Teluetteham* 1086 (Domesday Book), *Theluetham* c.1095, *Thelnetham* 1254. Possibly 'the swan enclosure or river-meadow by the plank bridge', from Old English *elfitu* 'swan' and *hamm* with *thel* 'a wooden plank or board'. As in W(h)elnetham, the early change from *-uet-* (representing *-vet-*) to *-net-* is due to scribal confusion between *u* and *n*. The local pronunciation is 'thelneeth'm'.

Thingoe Hill (in Bury St Edmunds)   Once the meeting-place of the medieval Hundred of Thingoe, recorded as *Thinghowe* 1042-66 (in a 14th century copy of an Anglo-Saxon charter), *Thingehov*, *Tingov* 1086 (Domesday Book), *Thingowe* 1254, 'the assembly mound', from Old Scandinavian *thing-haugr*.

Thorington   *Torentuna, Tornintuna, Turnintuna* 1086 (Domesday Book), *Thurintone* 1254. 'The farmstead or estate where thorn-trees grow', from Old English *thorn* or *thyrne* and *tūn*.

Thorington Street (near Stoke-by-Nayland)   Marked thus on Hodskinson's map of 1783 and on the Ordnance Survey map of 1805, no doubt identical in origin and meaning with the previous name, with the addition of *street* in the sense 'hamlet'.

Thorndon   *Torn(e)duna* 1086 (Domesday Book), *Thorndune* c.1095. 'The hill where thorn-trees grow', from Old English *thorn* and *dūn*.

Thorney Green (near Stowmarket)   *Tornei(a), Tornai* 1086 (Domesday Book), *Thorneie, Thorney* 13th century. 'The island (of dry or higher ground) where thorn-trees grow', from Old English *thorn* and *ēg*, later with *green* 'village green, hamlet'.

Thornham Magna & Parva   *T(h)ornham, Marthorham, paruo Thornham* 1086 (Domesday Book), *Magna Thornham* 1235. 'The homestead or village where thorn-trees grow', from Old English *thorn* and *hām*. The distinguishing affixes are Latin *magna* 'great' (replacing Old English *māra* 'greater') and *parva* 'little'. Thornham in Norfolk is identical in origin and meaning.

Thorpe (near Ashfield), *see* Ashfield cum Thorpe.

Thorpe Common (near Trimley St Martin)   *Torpa* 1086 (Domesday Book), *Torp* 1202, *Thorp* 1327. Identical in origin with the following names.

Thorpe Green   Marked thus on Hodskinson's map of 1783 and on the Ordnance Survey map of 1837, named from Thorpe Morieux, with *green* 'village green, hamlet'.

Thorpe Hall (near Hasketon)   Marked thus on the Ordnance Survey map of 1805, named from *Torp* 1086 (Domesday Book), identical with the following names.

Thorpe Morieux   *Thorp* 962-91 (in an 11th century copy of an Anglo-Saxon will), *Torp(a)* 1086 (Domesday Book), *Thorp Morieux* 1330. From

Old Scandinavian *thorp* 'outlying farmstead or hamlet, dependent secondary settlement', with later manorial affix from the family of Roger *de Morious*, here in 1201. The family took their name from Morieux near St Brieuc in Brittany. The local pronunciation is 'thorp-m'roo'.

Thorpeness *Torp* 1086 (Domesday Book), *Thorp* 1275. From Old Scandinavian *thorp* as in the previous name, with the later addition of *ness* (Old English *næss*, Old Scandinavian *nes*) 'headland, promontory'. The Meare here (fed by Hundred River) is marked as *The Mear* on Hodskinson's map of 1783, from *mere* 'a lake'.

Thorp Hall (in Dallinghoo) Marked thus on the Ordnance Survey map of 1837, named from *Torp* 1086 (Domesday Book), identical in origin with the previous names.

Thrandeston *Thrandeston c.*1035 (in a 13th century copy of an Anglo-Saxon will), *Thrandestuna, Thrundestuna* 1086 (Domesday Book). 'The farmstead or estate of a man called Thrándr', from Old English *tūn* and an Old Scandinavian personal name.

Thurleston (near Westerfield) *Toroluestuna, Turoluestuna* 1086 (Domesday Book), *Thurleston* 1254. 'The farmstead or estate of a man called Thórulfr', from Old English *tūn* and an Old Scandinavian personal name. The local pronunciation is 'thurl-st'n'.

Thurlow, Great & Little *Tridlauua, Tritlauua, Thrillauura* 1086 (Domesday Book), *Trillawe Magna, Trillawe Parva* 1254. Probably 'the hill or burial mound of the warriors', from Old English *thrȳth* 'a troop of warriors' and *hlāw*. Alternatively the first element may be Old English **thride* 'deliberation', thus 'the hill or mound used for meetings or assemblies'.

Thurston (near Bury St Edmunds) *Thurstuna, Torstuna* 1086 (Domesday Book), *Thurstune c.*1095. 'The farmstead or estate of a man called Thóri or Thúr', from Old English *tūn* and an Old Scandinavian personal name.

Thurston End (near Hawkedon) *Thurstanestuna* 1086 (Domesday Book), *Turstaneston c.*1145. 'The farmstead or estate of a man called Thorsteinn', from Old English *tūn* and an Old Scandinavian personal name. It is marked *Thurston End* on Hodskinson's map of 1783, from *end* 'district of a parish, hamlet'.

Thwaite *Theyt* 1228, *Thueyt*, *Tweyt* 13th century. From Old Scandinavian *thveit* 'a woodland clearing, a meadow, a paddock'. The local pronunciation is 'thwate' or 'twate'. Thwaite St Mary in Norfolk is identical in origin and meaning.

Timworth *Timeworda*, *Timwrtha* 1086 (Domesday Book), *Timeworthe* 1166. 'The enclosure or enclosed farmstead of a man called *Tima', from Old English *worth* and an Old English personal name. **Timworth Green** is marked thus on the Ordnance Survey map of 1836, from *green* 'village green, hamlet'.

Tostock *Totestoc*, *Totstocha* 1086 (Domesday Book), *Totestok* 1226-8. 'The outlying farmstead or hamlet by the look-out place', from Old English *tōt and *stoc*.

Trimley St Martin & St Mary *Tremelaia*, *Tremlega* 1086 (Domesday Book), *Tremele Sancti Martini*, *Tremle Beate Marie* 1254. 'The woodland clearing of a man called *Trymma', from Old English *lēah* and an Old English personal name. The distinguishing affixes (Latin in the 13th century spellings) are from the dedications of the churches.

Troston *Trostingtun* 975-1016 (Anglo-Saxon will), *Trostuna* 1086 (Domesday Book). Hitherto explained as 'the farmstead or estate associated with a man called *Trost(a)', from an Old English personal name with medial connective *-ing-* ('called after') and *tūn*. However a recent suggestion that the first element is rather an Anglo-Scandinavian personal name *Trōsting* is to be preferred.

Tuddenham (near Mildenhall) *Tode(n)ham*, *Totenham* 1086 (Domesday Book), *Tudenham* 1235. Identical in origin and meaning with the following name.

Tuddenham St Martin (near Ipswich) *Tude(n)ham*, *Toddenham* 1086 (Domesday Book), *Tudenham* 1280. 'The homestead or village of a man called Tud(d)a', from an Old English personal name (genitive case *-an*) and Old English *hām*. The distinguishing affix is from the dedication of the church. The local pronunciation is 'tud'n'm'. The previous name as well as East & North Tuddenham in Norfolk are identical in origin and meaning.

Tunstall *Tunestal* 1086 (Domesday Book), *Tunstall* 1242. From Old English *tūn-stall* 'the site of a farm, a farmstead'. Tunstall in Norfolk and other counties has the same origin and meaning.

Ubbeston Green *Upbestuna* 1086 (Domesday Book), *Ubbeston* 1206. 'The farmstead or estate of a man called Ubbi', from Old English *tūn* and an Old Scandinavian personal name. *Ubbeston Green* is marked thus on Hodskinson's map of 1783, from *green* 'village green, hamlet'. The local pronunciation is 'ubber-st'n'.

Ufford *Uffeworda, Offeworda, Uffeforda* 1086 (Domesday Book), *Ufford* 1195. Perhaps originally 'the enclosure or enclosed farmstead of a man called Uffa', from an Old English personal name and Old English *worth*, but this word clearly alternated with, or was replaced by, Old English *ford* 'a ford' at an early date. There is a crossing of the River Deben here. The local pronunciation is 'uff'd'.

Uggeshall *Uggiceheala, Uggecehala* 1086 (Domesday Book), *Ugechale, Ugeshale* 1254. 'The nook of land or hollow of a man called *Uggeca', from an Old English personal name and Old English *halh*. The local pronunciation is 'ugga-shawl' or 'ugga-sh'l'.

Ulveston Hall (in Debenham) *Uluestuna, Uluestune* 1086 (Domesday Book), *Uluestone* 1327. 'The farmstead or estate of a man called Ulfr', from Old English *tūn* and an Old Scandinavian personal name.

Wade (near Barnby) *Wada* 1165, *Wade* 1205. From Old English *(ge)wæd* 'a ford', referring to a crossing of the River Waveney which flows just to the north of here.

Walberswick *Walberdeswike* 1199, *Walberteswyk* 1275. 'The harbour or trading centre of a man called Walbert', from Old English *wīc* and a Continental Germanic personal name.

Waldingfield, Great & Little *Wæaldingafæld, Wealdingafeld* 962-91 (in 11th and 13th century copies of an Anglo-Saxon will), *Waldingefelda* 1086 (Domesday Book), *Waldingfeud Magna, Waudingefeud Parva* 1254. 'The open land of the forest dwellers', from Old English *w(e)ald* with *-inga-* (genitive case of *-ingas* 'people of') and *feld*. There are still remnants of ancient woodland in surrounding parishes. The early distinguishing affixes are Latin *magna* 'great' and *parva* 'little'. The local pronunciation is 'wall-dingfield' (with the stress on the first syllable).

Waldringfield *Waldringfeld* c.946 (in a 13th century copy of an Anglo-Saxon will), *Waldringafelda* 1086 (Domesday Book). 'The open land of the family or followers of a man called Waldhere', from an Old English personal name with *-inga-* (genitive case of *-ingas* 'people of') and *feld*. The local pronunciation is 'wall-dringfield' (with the stress on the first syllable).

Walpole *Walepola* 1086 (Domesday Book), *Walepol* 1254. 'The pool of the Britons', from Old English *walh* (genitive case plural *wala*) and *pōl*. The pool lay in a confluence of the River Blyth and a tributary, and the village itself lies just two miles south of the Roman villa site at Chediston. This name and the next two names are particularly interesting and significant because they indicate some survival of a British element in the population of these areas in the Anglo-Saxon period.

Walsham le Willows *Wal(e)sam* 1086 (Domesday Book), *Walesham* 1203. 'The homestead or village of a man called Walh', from an Old English personal name and *hām*. The personal name means 'the Briton or Welshman'. The affix *le Willows* (meaning 'among the willow-trees'), first noted on the Ordnance Survey map of 1836, distinguishes this place from North & South Walsham in Norfolk, which have the same origin.

Walton *Wealtune* 975-1016 (Anglo-Saxon will), *Waletuna* 1086 (Domesday Book), *Waleton* 1159. 'The farmstead or estate of the Britons', from Old English *walh* (genitive case plural *wala*) and *tūn*. For *Walton Castle* (re-fortified in the 12th century on the site of a Roman fort and now lost to the sea), *see* Felixstowe. Walton on the Naze in Essex is identical in origin and meaning.

Wangford (near Lakenheath) *Waineforda*, *Wamforda* 1086 (Domesday Book), *Waineford* 1190. 'The ford usable by wagons or carts', from Old English *wægn* (genitive case plural *wægna*) and *ford*. The ford was at a crossing of the Little Ouse River.

Wangford (near Southwold) *Wankeforda* 1086 (Domesday Book), *Wangeford* 1238. Probably 'the ford by the open fields', from Old English *wang* (genitive case plural *wanga*) 'open ground' and *ford*. The ford was at a crossing of a tributary of the River Blyth.

Wantisden (near Butley) *Wantesdena* 1086 (Domesday Book), *Wantesdene* 1254. 'The valley of a man called Want', from Old English *denu* and an Old English personal name.

Washbrook *Wasebroc* 1198, *Wassebroc* 1254. 'The brook used for washing (sheep or clothes)', or 'the brook liable to flood', from Old English *brōc* with either *wæsce* or *(ge)wæsc*.

Wattisfield *Watlesfelda, Watefelda* 1086 (Domesday Book), *Watlesfeld c.*1150. Probably 'the open land of a man called *Wætel or *Hwætel', from Old English *feld* and an Old English personal name.

Wattisham *Wecesham* 1086 (Domesday Book), *Wachesham* 1184. 'The homestead or village of a man called *Wæcci', from Old English *hām* and an Old English personal name.

Waveney (district), named from the **River Waveney** which is *Wahenhe* 1275, *Wagenho* 1286, 'the quagmire river', from Old English **wagen* and *ēa*. This great river forms the ancient boundary between the northern East Angles of Norfolk and the southern East Angles of Suffolk.

Welnetham, Great & Little (sometimes spelt Whelnetham) *Telueteham, Hvelfi(t)ham* 1086 (Domesday Book), *Weluetham* 1170, *Welnetham* 1206. Possibly 'the swan enclosure or river-meadow by the waterwheel or other circular feature', from Old English *elfitu* 'swan' and *hamm* with *hwēol* 'wheel'. As in Thelnetham (which may also be from Old English *elfethamm* with a different prefix), the early change from -*uet-* (representing -*vet-*) to -*net-* is due to the scribal confusion of *u* and *n*. The local pronunciation is 'wellneeth'm' (with the stress on the second syllable).

Wenham, Great & Little *Wenham* 1086 (Domesday Book), *Parva Wenham* 1242-3, *Magna Wenham* 1327. Possibly 'the homestead or village with pastureland', from Old English **wynn* and *hām*. Alternatively the first element may be Old English *wenn* 'a tumour' (used for 'a hillock or hill-spur'). The early distinguishing affixes are Latin *magna* 'great' and *parva* 'little'.

Wenhaston *Wenadestuna* 1086 (Domesday Book), *Wenhaueston* 1197. 'The farmstead or estate of a man called *Wynhæth', from Old English *tūn* and an

94

Old English personal name. The local pronunciation is 'wenner-st'n'.

Wentford (near Clare) *Wanteford* 1315. 'The ford on a path or track', from Middle English *wente* and *ford*. The name refers to a crossing of Chilton Stream.

Westerfield *Westrefelda* 1086 (Domesday Book), *Westerfeld* 1206. 'The (more) westerly open land', from Old English **wester* or *westerra* and *feld*. Perhaps named in relation to Waldringfield.

Westhall *Westhala* 1169, *Westhale* 1212. 'The western hollow or nook of land', from Old English *west* and *halh* (dative case *hale*). Probably named in relation to Uggeshall. The local pronunciation is 'west'l'.

Westhorpe *Westtorp*, *Westurp* 1086 (Domesday Book), *Westhorpe* 1285. 'The westerly outlying farmstead or hamlet', from Old English *west* and Old Scandinavian *thorp*.

Westleton *Westledestuna*, *Weslestuna* 1086 (Domesday Book), *Westleton* 1202. 'The farmstead or estate of a man called Vestlithi', from Old English *tūn* and an Old Scandinavian personal name (a byname meaning 'traveller to the west' and denoting a warrior who went west on Viking expeditions). The local pronunciation is 'wessel-t'n'.

Westley *Westlea* 1086 (Domesday Book), *Uuestlea* c.1095. 'The westerly woodland clearing', from Old English *west* and *lēah*. It lies to the west of Bury St Edmunds.

Weston (near Beccles) *Westuna* 1086 (Domesday Book), *Weston* 1212. 'The west farmstead or estate', from Old English *west* and *tūn*, perhaps so named in relation to Ellough.

Weston, Coney, *see* Coney Weston.

Weston, Market *Westuna* 1086 (Domesday Book), *Weston* 1202, *Market Weston* 1783. 'The west farmstead or estate', from Old English *west* and *tūn*, with the later affix referring to the important early market (the right to have a market here was granted in 1263). Perhaps named in relation to Thelnetham.

West Row Marked thus on Hodskinson's map of 1783 and on the Ordnance Survey map of 1836, from Middle English *rowe* 'row of houses, hamlet', so named from its situation west of Mildenhall.

West Stow, *see* Stow.

Wetherden *Wederdena* 1086 (Domesday Book), *Wetherden* 1197. 'The valley where wether-sheep are kept', from Old English *wether* and *denu*.

Wetheringsett *Weddreringesete* 1017-35, *Wetheringsete* 1043-5 (in 12th and 13th century copies of Anglo-Saxon wills), *Wederingaseta* 1086 (Domesday Book). Probably 'the fold(s) of the people of Wetherden', from a reduced form of the previous name with Old English *-inga-* (genitive case of *-ingas* 'dwellers at') and *set* 'a fold or stable for animals'. The local pronunciation is 'wethringset'.

Weybread *Weibrada*, *Weibrade* 1086 (Domesday Book), *Weiebred c.*1200. 'The broad stretch of land by the road', from Old English *weg* and *brǣdu*. The name refers to the Roman road running through here north-west towards the River Waveney. The local pronunciation is 'way-br'd'.

Whatfield *Wate(s)felda* 1086 (Domesday Book), *Whatefeld* 1205. 'The open land where wheat is grown', from Old English *hwǣte* and *feld*.

Whelnetham, *see* Welnetham.

Whepstead *Wepstede c.*946 (in a 13th century copy of an Anglo-Saxon will), *Hwipstede* 975-1016 (Anglo-Saxon will), *Huepestede* 1086 (Domesday Book). Probably 'the place where brushwood grows', from Old English **hwip(p)e* and *stede*.

Wherstead *Weruesteda* 1086 (Domesday Book), *Warvestede* 1207. 'The place by the wharf or shore', from Old English *hwearf* and *stede*, no doubt with reference to an early landing place on the River Orwell just down river from Ipswich. The local pronunciation is 'ware-st'd'.

Whittingham Green, Little (near Fressingfield) *Wytingham c.*1035 (in a 13th century copy of an Anglo-Saxon will), *Wettingaham* 1086 (Domesday Book). 'The homestead of the family or followers of a man called Witta', from an Old

English personal name with *-inga-* (genitive case of *-ingas* 'people of') and *hām*.

Whitton *Widituna* 1086 (Domesday Book), *Witton* 1212, *Wytenton* mid-13th century. 'The farmstead or estate associated with a man called Hwīta', from an Old English personal name with medial connective *-ing-* ('called after') and *tūn*.

Wickhambrook *Wicham* 1086 (Domesday Book), *Wichambrok* 1254. 'The homestead or village associated with a *vicus*, i.e. an earlier Romano-British settlement', from Old English *wīc-hām*, as also in the following two names, here with the later addition of Old English *brōc* 'a brook or stream'. A large Roman villa has been discovered at nearby Lidgate. The local pronunciation is 'wick'm-bruk'.

Wickham Market *Wikham* 1086 (Domesday Book), *Wicham* 1254, *Wickhammarket* 1377. Identical in origin and meaning with the previous name. The etymology is confirmed by the discovery of a large Roman settlement just north of the present town. The later distinguishing affix refers to the important early market here (in use in 1377).

Wickham Skeith *Wichamm* 1086 (Domesday Book), *Wicham Skeyth* 1368. From Old English *wīc-hām* like the previous names. This place lies on a Roman road and near a small Roman settlement. The unusual affix, from Old Scandinavian *skeith* 'a race-course (for horses)', is interesting: both horse-racing and horse-fighting were popular among the Vikings, especially at their heathen feasts. The local pronunciation is 'wick'm skeeth'.

Wilby *Wilebey*, *Wilebi* 1086 (Domesday Book), *Wylebeye* 1254. 'The circle of willow-trees', from Old English **wilig* and *bēag* 'a ring'.

Wilford Bridge (near Melton) Marked thus on Hodskinson's map of 1783, named from *Wileforde* 1086 (Domesday Book), 1254. 'The willow-tree ford', from Old English *wilig* and *ford*, with reference to an important crossing of the River Deben: indeed the bridge (replacing the earlier ford) is the lowest crossing of the river to its mouth some ten miles downstream. The place also gave its name to a medieval Hundred, the meetings of which were no doubt once held at the ford.

Willingham St Mary (near Sotterley)   *Willingaham, Wellingaham* 1086 (Domesday Book), *Willingeham* 1188. 'The homestead of the family or followers of a man called Willa', from an Old English personal name with *-inga-* (genitive case of *-ingas* 'people of') and Old English *hām*. Cherry Willingham and South Willingham in Lincolnshire are identical in origin and meaning.

Willisham Tye   *Willauesham* 1035-44 (in a 13th century copy of an Anglo-Saxon will), 1176. 'The homestead or village of a man called Wīglāf', from Old English *hām* and an Old English personal name. Tye is dialect *tye* (from Old English *tēag*) 'a large common pasture', as in other south Suffolk names.

Wingfield   *Wingefeld* c.1035 (in a 13th century copy of an Anglo-Saxon will), *Wighefelda* 1086 (Domesday Book), *Wihingefeld* 1185. Probably 'the open land of the family or followers of a man called *Wiga', from an Old English personal name with *-inga-* (genitive case of *-ingas* 'people of') and *feld*. Alternatively the first element may be Old English *wīg* 'a heathen temple', thus 'the open land of the temple people'.

Winston   *Winestuna* 1086 (Domesday Book), *Wyneston, Wineston* late 13th century. 'The farmstead or estate of a man called Wine', from Old English *tūn* and an Old English personal name.

Wissett   *Wisseta, Uuitsede* 1086 (Domesday Book), *Witseta* 1165. Possibly 'the fold(s) of a man called Witta', from an Old English personal name and *set* (plural *setu*) 'a fold or stable for animals'.

Wissington   *Wiswythetun* 1000-2 (in an 11th century copy of an Anglo-Saxon will), *Wisinton* 1242. 'The farmstead or estate of a woman called Wīgswīth', from Old English *tūn* and an Old English personal name. This is one of the four Suffolk places named from an Anglo-Saxon female landowner. The local pronunciation is 'wissing-t'n' or (older) 'wiss-t'n'.

Withermarsh Green (near Polstead) *Hwifermirsc, Wifærmyrsc* late 10th century (in 11th century copies of Anglo-Saxon wills), *Withermers* 1086 (Domesday Book), *Wivermers* 1219. From Old English *mersc* 'a marsh' with an uncertain first element, apparently an Old English adjective **hwifer* or *wifer* meaning 'unstable, shaking' (thus referring to swampy ground). *Withermarsh Green* is marked thus on Hodskinson's map of 1783, with *green* 'village green, hamlet'.

98

Withersdale Street *Weresdel* [sic] 1086 (Domesday Book), *Wideresdala* 1184, *Wetheresdale* 1254. Etymology uncertain. Possibly 'the valley where wether-sheep are kept', from Old English *wether* and *dæl*. Alternatively perhaps 'the valley of a man called Vítharr', from Old Scandinavian *dalr* and an Old Scandinavian personal name. The later addition *street* (as on the Ordnance Survey map of 1836) has the sense 'street of houses, hamlet'.

Withersfield *Wedresfelda*, *Vrdresfelda* [sic, for *Vedresfelda*] 1086 (Domesday Book), *Wetherisfeud* 1254. 'The open land where wether-sheep are kept', from Old English *wether* and *feld*.

Witnesham *Witdesham* [sic] 1086 (Domesday Book), *Witnesham* 1254. Probably 'the homestead or village of a man called *Wittīn', from Old English *hām* and an Old English personal name. The local pronunciation is 'witner-sh'm'.

Wixoe *Wlteskeou* [sic, ? for *Witkeseou*] 1086 (Domesday Book), *Widekeshoo* 1205. 'The hill-spur of a man called Widuc', from an Old English personal name and Old English *hōh*.

Woodbridge *Oddebruge* 1042-66 (in a 12th century copy of an Anglo-Saxon charter), *Wudebrige*, *Wudebryge* 1086 (Domesday Book). 'The wooden bridge', or 'the bridge near the wood', from Old English *wudu* and *brycg*.

Woolpit *Wlpit* c.1000 (in a 13th century copy of an Anglo-Saxon charter), *Wlfpeta* 1086 (Domesday Book), *Wulpettas* 11th century. 'The pit(s) for trapping wolves', from Old English *wulf-pytt* (plural *-pyttas*).

Woolverstone *Uluerestuna*, *Hulferestuna* 1086 (Domesday Book), *Wolferston* 1196. 'The farmstead or estate of a man called Wulfhere', from Old English *tūn* and an Old English personal name. The local pronunciation is 'wulver-st'n'.

Wootten Green (near Stradbroke) Marked as *Wotting Green* on Hodskinson's map of 1783, and as *Wooton Green* on the Ordnance Survey map of 1837, named from *Wotton* 1275, 'the farmstead or estate in or near a wood', from Old English *wudu* and *tūn*.

Wordwell (near West Stow) *Wridewellan* c.1040 (Anglo-Saxon charter), *Wridewella* 1086 (Domesday Book). Probably 'the winding stream', from Old

English *wride 'a twist, a bend' and *wella*, with reference to the River Lark near which the place lies, *see* also Worlington.

Worlingham *Werlingaham*, *Warlingaham* 1086 (Domesday Book), *Werlingeham* 1168. Probably 'the homestead of the family or followers of a man called *Wērel', from an Old English personal name with *-inga-* (genitive case of *-ingas* 'people of') and Old English *hām*. The local pronunciation is 'wurling'm'.

Worlington *Wirilintona* 1086 (Domesday Book), *Wridelingeton* 1201. Probably 'the farmstead or estate near the winding stream', from Old English *wride* and *wella* with medial connective *-ing-* ('associated with') and *tūn*. Alternatively perhaps 'the farmstead of those living by the winding stream', from Old English *-inga-* (genitive case of *-ingas* 'people of'). In either case, the reference is to its situation on the River Lark, *see* also Wordwell which lies some 7 miles east. The local pronunciation is 'wurling-t'n'.

Worlingworth *Wilrincgawertha* c.1035 (Anglo-Saxon will), *Wyrlingwortha* 1086 (Domesday Book). 'The enclosure or enclosed farmstead of the family or followers of a man called Wilhere', from an Old English personal name with *-inga-* (genitive case of *-ingas* 'people of') and Old English *worth*. The local pronunciation is 'wurling-w'th'.

Wortham *Wrtham* c.946 (in a 13th century copy of an Anglo-Saxon will), *Wortham*, *Word(h)am* 1086 (Domesday Book). 'The homestead or village with an enclosure', from Old English *worth* and *hām*. The local pronunciation is 'wurth'm'.

Wratting, Great & Little *Wratinga* 1086 (Domesday Book), *Uurartinge* 11th century, *Wretting*, *Wrotting* 1206. 'The place where crosswort or hellebore grows', from Old English *wrætt* with suffix *-ing*. West Wratting in Cambridgeshire is identical in origin and meaning.

Wren, River (flowing into Easton Broad to the north of Southwold), *see* Wrentham.

Wrentham *Wretham*, *Uuereteham* [sic] 1086 (Domesday Book), *Wrentham* 1228. Probably 'the homestead or village of a man called *Wrenta', from Old

English *hām* and an Old English personal name. The local pronunciation is 'ren-th'm'. The river-name **Wren** is apparently a so-called back-formation from the place-name (thus complementing the other Suffolk streams named from birds, *see* Dove, Lark and Linnet).

Wyken Hall (in Bardwell) *Wica, Wicam* 1086 (Domesday Book), *Wykes, Wicen* 1414. 'The dwellings, the specialized farm or trading settlement', from Old English *wīc* (dative case plural *wīcum*, Middle English plural *wikes* and *wiken*). The *-am* in the second Domesday Book form (simply an inflection) has been wrongly taken by some earlier commentators to indicate an origin from Old English *wīc-hām*. Wicken in Cambridgeshire and Wicken Bonhunt in Essex are identical in origin and meaning

Wyverstone *Wiuerthestuna, Wiuerdestuna* 1086 (Domesday Book), *Wiverdeston* 1203. 'The farmstead or estate of a man called Wīgferth', from Old English *tūn* and an Old English personal name. The local pronunciation is 'wyver-st'n'.

Yaxley *Jacheslea, Iacheslea* 1086 (Domesday Book), *Iakeslea* 1170. 'The wood or woodland clearing of the cuckoo', from Old English *gēac* (genitive case *-es*) and Old English *lēah*.

Yoxford *Gokesford, Iokesfort* 1086 (Domesday Book), *Iokesford* 1254. 'The ford wide enough for a yoke of oxen', from Old English *geoc* and *ford*. The river-name **Yox** is a so-called back-formation from the place-name.

GLOSSARY OF THE ELEMENTS
FOUND IN SUFFOLK PLACE-NAMES

In this list, OE stands for Old English (the English language *c*.450-*c*.1100), ME for Middle English (*c*.1100-*c*.1500), ModE for Modern English (*c*.1500 to the present day), OFr for Old French, and OScand. for Old Scandinavian (the language of the Vikings, comprising Old Danish and Old Norse). The Old English letters 'thorn' and 'eth' have been rendered *th* throughout. The Old English letter *æ* represents a sound between *a* and *e*. Elements with an asterisk are postulated or hypothetical forms, that is they are words not recorded in independent use or only found in use at a later date.

āc OE 'oak-tree'. Copdock, Oakley, Occold.

æcer OE 'plot of cultivated or arable land'. Benacre, Chadacre.

æsc OE 'ash-tree'. Ashbocking, Ashfield (x 4), Ash Street, Campsea Ashe, Dodnash, Stoke Ash.

æspe OE 'aspen-tree'. Aspall.

ætheling OE 'prince'. Athelington.

alor OE 'alder-tree'. Alderton.

*amal Celtic 'edge, boundary. ?*Amalburnan* (*see* River Box).

āmynni OScand. 'river-mouth'. Minsmere Haven.

āna OE 'single, lonely'. Onehouse.

askr OScand. 'ash-tree'. Ashby.

bæc OE 'ridge'. ?Debach.

*balg OE 'rounded'. ?Ballingdon.

barn OScand. 'child, heir'. ?Barnby.

beacon ModE. Beacon Hill.

bēan OE 'bean'. Benacre.

bēanen OE 'growing with beans'. Benhall Green.

bēag OE 'ring, circle'. Wilby.

bearu OE 'wood, grove'. Barrow.

bece OE, 'stream, valley'. Beccles, ?Debach, Gosbeck.

beck ME (from OScand. **bekkr**) 'small stream, brook'. The Beck, Beck Row.

*begel OE 'river-bend'. Baylham.

bēl OE 'fire, funeral pyre, beacon'. ?Bealings, ?Belstead, ?Belton.

*bel OE 'glade, dry ground in marsh'. ?Bealings, ?Belstead, ?Belton.

beonet OE 'bent-grass'. Bentley.

beorg OE 'rounded hill, mound, tumulus'. Babergh, Barham, Bergholt, Chedburgh, Finborough, Kettleburgh.

beorht OE 'bright, clear'. Brightwell.

beorn OE 'warrior'. ?Barnham.

bere-tūn, bær-tūn OE 'barley farm, corn farm, grange or demesne farm'. Great Barton, Barton Mills.

blæc OE 'black, dark-coloured'. The Black Bourn, Blackheath, Blackthorpe.

blīthe OE 'gentle, pleasant'. River Blyth (in Blyford and Blythburgh).

*boia OE 'boy, servant'. ?Boyton (x 2).

bōc OE 'beech-tree'. ?Boxted.

bouge OFr 'uncultivated land covered with heather'. ?Boulge.

box OE 'box-tree'. Boxford, ?Boxted.

brād OE 'broad, spacious'. Bradfield, Bradley, Bradwell, Broad Green.

brǣdu OE 'plain, broad piece of land'. Bredfield, Weybread.

brant OE 'steep'. ?Brantham.

breck ModE dialect (from OE **brēc, brǣc**) 'land broken up for cultivation'. Breckland.

brend ME 'burnt'. Bradfield Combust, Brent Eleigh.

brīosa OE 'gadfly'. ?Braiseworth, Great Bricett.

broad ModE 'extensive piece of water'. Oulton Broad.

brōc OE 'brook, stream'. ?Brockford Street, ?Brockley (x 2), Holbrook, Rushbrooke, Stradbroke, Washbrook, Wickhambrook.

brocc OE 'badger'. ?Brockford Street, ?Brockley (x 2).

brōm OE 'thorny bush, broom'. Bramfield, Bramford, Brampton, Brandon, Brome, Bromeswell, Brundon.

brunnr OScand. 'spring, stream'. ?Newbourne.

brycg OE 'bridge'. East Bridge, Wilford Bridge, Woodbridge.

bucc OE 'buck (male deer or he-goat)'. ?Buxhall, ?Buxlow Manor.

bula OE 'bull'. Bulcamp.

*bung OE 'swelling, lump'. Bungay.

būr OE, **bower** ME 'dwelling, cottage' later 'arbour, bower, shelter'. Bower House Tye, Bures.

(ge)būr OE 'peasant holding land for rent or services'. Bruisyard.

burh (dative **byrig**) OE 'fortress, stronghold, fortified town or manor'. Aldeburgh, Blythburgh, *Burg* (*see* Felixstowe), Burgate, Burgh, Burgh Castle, Bury St Edmunds, Grundisburgh, Rumburgh, Sudbury.

burh-stall OE 'site of a fortress or stronghold'. Burstall.

burna OE 'spring, stream'. Alnesbourn, *Amalburnan* (*see* River Box), The Black Bourn, Brundish, ?Newbourne, Sudbourne.

bushe ME (from OE **busc**) 'bush, thicket'. Buss Creek.

*butt OE 'tree-trunk, log'. ?Butley.

bý OScand. 'farmstead, village, settlement'. Ashby, Barnby, Risby.

*bysce OE, ***byski** OScand. 'bushy copse, scrubland'. Bixley.

cærse OE 'cress, water-cress'. Kersey, ?Kesgrave.

camb OE 'hill-crest, ridge'. Combs.

camp OE 'field, enclosure'. Bulcamp, Campsea Ashe.

capel ME (OFr) 'chapel'. Capel St Andrew, Capel St Mary.

castel ME 'castle'. Burgh Castle.

catt OE 'cat, wild-cat'. Cattawade, ?Cattishall.

*cearr OE 'turn, bend'. Stanton Chare.

ceorl OE 'freeman, peasant'. ?Chelsworth.

ceosol OE 'gravel'. Chillesford.

cert OE 'patch of rough or wooded ground'. Chadacre.

cetel OE 'deep valley'. Kettleburgh.

cild OE 'child, youth, younger son, young nobleman'. Chilton (x 3).

clǣgig OE 'clayey'. Claydon.

clopp(a) OE 'lump, hill'. Clopton (x 2).

*cnott OE 'hillock'. ?Knodishall.

cofa OE 'shelter, chamber, cave, cove'. North & South Cove.

cold ModE (OE **cald**) 'cold'. Coldfair Green.

combust ME (from Latin *combusta*) 'burnt'. Bradfield Combust, Brent Eleigh.

coninger ME 'rabbit-warren'. Conyer's Green.

*coppod OE 'with top removed, pollarded'. Copdock.

corn OE 'corn'. Cornard.

corner ModE. Clopton Corner.

*cors Celtic 'marsh, fen'. Cosford.

cran OE 'crane'. Cranley, Cransford.

creek ModE 'inlet'. Buss Creek, Martlesham Creek.

croft OE 'enclosure, small enclosed field'. St Cross South Elmham.

croh OE 'nook, corner'. Crowfield.

cross ModE 'cross-roads'. Bell's Cross.

cucu OE 'cuckoo'. ?Cookley.

cyne- OE 'royal'. ?Kenton.

cyning OE 'king'. King's Fleet, Kingston.

dæl OE 'hollow, valley'. Botesdale, Dalham, ?Withersdale Street.

dalr OScand. 'valley'. ?Withersdale Street.

denu OE 'valley'. Denham (x 2), Depden, Elveden, Framsden, Frostenden, Hundon, Monewden, Ousden, Rattlesden, Shadingfield, Wantisden, Wetherden.

dēop OE 'deep'. Depden.

dēope OE 'the deep one'. Debenham, Debach.

dūn OE 'low hill, down'. Ballingdon, Brandon, Brundon, Claydon, Darmsden, Dunwich, Hawkedon, Raydon, Reydon, Santon Downham, Thorndon.

ēa OE 'river, stream'. Groton, Waveney.

(e)ald OE 'old, disused'. Aldeburgh, ?Aldham, Old Newton.

ealh OE 'heathen temple'. ?Ellough.

ēast OE 'east, eastern'. Assington Green, East Bergholt, East Bridge, Easton, Easton Bavents.

edisc OE 'pasture, enclosure, enclosed park'. Brundish, Cavendish.

ēg OE 'island (of dry or higher ground in marsh), land partly surrounded by water, promontory'. Bawdsey, Bungay, Campsea Ashe, Eye, ?Hussey Green, Kersey, Lindsey, Thorney Green.

ēg-land OE 'island (of dry or higher ground)'. Nayland.

eik OScand. 'oak-tree'. Eyke.

elf OE 'elf, fairy'. ?Elveden.

elfitu OE 'swan'. ?Elveden, ?Thelnetham, ?Welnetham.

elm OE 'elm-tree'. Elmham, Elmswell.

__*elme__ OE 'elm wood'. Elmsett.

end ModE 'district or quarter of a parish, hamlet'. Assington Green, Boyton End, Grimstone End, Rotten End, Thurston End.

eorl OE 'nobleman, earl'. Earl Soham, Earl Stonham.

erth OE 'ploughed or cultivated land'. Cornard, Horringer/Horningsheath.

fearn OE 'fern, bracken'. Farnham.

feld OE 'open country, open land cleared of trees'. Ashfield (x 4), Badmondisfield Hall, Bedfield, Bedingfield, Bradfield, Bramfield, Bredfield, Charsfield, Cockfield, Cratfield, Crowfield, Fressingfield, Homersfield, Huntingfield, Huntingfield, Laxfield, Metfield, Mickfield, Pakefield, Redlingfield, Ringsfield, Shadingfield, Stanningfield, Stansfield, Sternfield, Waldingfield, Waldringfield, Wattisfield, Westerfield, Whatfield, Wingfield, Withersfield.

fen(e)kel ME 'fennel'. Fingal Street.

fīna OE 'woodpecker'. ?Finborough.

Fleming OE 'Fleming (native of Flanders)'. Flempton.

flēot OE 'inlet, creek, stream'. Herringfleet, King's Fleet.

folc OE 'folk, tribe, people'. Suffolk.

ford OE 'ford, river-crossing'. Battisford, Blyford, Boxford, Bramford, Brockford Street, Chillesford, ?Coldfair Green, Cosford, Cransford, Culford, *Finesforda* (*see* River Fynn), Fordley, Glemsford, Kentford, Lackford, Marlesford, Long Melford, Mutford, Orford, Playford, Seckford, Stratford (x 2), Ufford, Wangford (x 2), Wentford, Wilford, Yoxford.

forest ModE. Forest Heath.

forne OE 'trout'. Fornham.

forward ModE 'near, in front'. Forward Green.

fox-hol OE 'fox-hole, fox's earth'. Foxhall.

freca OE 'warrior'. ?Freckenham.

Frēsa, Frīsa OE 'a Frisian, a native of Friesland and the Frisian Isles'. Fressingfield, Freston, Friston.

Friday ModE. Friday Street.

frith OE 'safety, protection'. ?Fritton.

frosc OE 'frog'. Frostenden.

gāra OE 'gore, promontory'. Landguard.

gāt OE 'goat'. Gedgrave.

gēac OE 'cuckoo'. Yaxley.

geard OE 'yard, enclosure'. Bruisyard.

geat OE 'gate'. Burgate, Havergate.

geoc OE 'yoke (of oxen)'. Yoxford.

*gip(s), *gypes OE 'opening, gap'. ?Ipswich.

glēam OE 'revelry, games'. Glemham, Glemsford.

gnætt OE 'gnat'. ?Knettishall.

gōs OE 'goose'. Gosbeck.

græf OE 'pit, trench, ditch'. ?Kesgrave, ?Redgrave.

grāf(a) OE 'grove, copse, coppiced wood'. Gedgrave, Hargrave, ?Kesgrave, Palgrave, ?Redgrave.

*grēd OE 'grassy meadow'. Hengrave.

green (adjective) ModE. Greenstreet Green.

green (noun) ModE, **grene** ME 'grassy area, in particular a piece of public or common grazing land, a village green'. Frequent in names like Assington Green, Baxter's Green, Broad Green, Brockley Green, Chippenhall Green, etc.

grēot OE 'gravel'. Cretingham.

*groten OE 'gravelly, sandy'. Groton.

grund OE 'ground, foundation of a building'. ?Grundisburgh.

gull ModE dialect (**go(u)le** ME) 'channel, water-course'. The Gull.

hæfer OE 'he-goat'. Havergate Island, ?Haverhill.

*hæfera OE 'oats'. ?Haverhill.

hæsel OE 'hazel-tree'. Hazelwood.

hǣth OE 'heath, uncultivated land overgrown with heather and brushwood'. Blackheath, Forest Heath, Foxhall Heath, Hadleigh, Horringer, Leavenheath.

hafoc OE 'hawk'. ?Hawkedon.

haga OE 'hawthorn, hedge, hedged enclosure'. Haughley, Pettaugh.

hālig OE 'holy'. ?Holwell Row.

halh OE 'nook or corner of land, land in a hollow or river-bend, dry ground in marsh', also 'detached unit of land or estate'. Aspall, Benhall Green, Blaxhall, Buxhall, Cattishall, Chippenhall Green, Ilketshall, Kelsale, Knettishall, Knodishall, Mildenhall, ?*Northales* (*see* Covehithe), Peasenhall, Rickinghall, ?Ringshall, Spexhall, Uggeshall, Westhall.

hals OE 'spit of land'. ?*Northales* (*see* Covehithe).

hām OE 'homestead, village, manor, estate'. Akenham, Aldham, Aldringham, Badingham, Barham, Barnham, Barningham, Barsham, ?Baylham, Benningham, Blakenham, ?Brantham, Brettenham, Bucklesham, Cavenham, Chattisham, Coddenham, Cretingham, Dalham, Darsham, Debenham, Denham (x 2), Elmham, Fakenham, Falkenham, ?Farnham, Felsham, Finningham, Fornham, Framlingham, Freckenham, Gisleham, Gislingham, Glemham, Helmingham, Henham, Heveningham, Higham (x 2), Hintlesham, ?Hitcham, ?Horham, Icklingham, Ingham, Langham, Lavenham, Layham, Letheringham, Loudham, Martlesham, Mendham, Mendlesham, Mettingham, Needham Market, Needham Street, Pakenham, ?Parham, Redisham, Rendham, Rendlesham, Rougham Green, Santon Downham, Saxham, Saxmundham, Shottisham, Soham, Somersham, Stonham, Syleham, ?Tangham, Thornham, Tuddenham (x 2), Walsham le Willows, Wattisham, Wenham, Whittingham, Willingham, Willisham Tye, Witnesham, Worlingham, Wortham, Wrentham.

hamm OE 'enclosure, land hemmed in by water or marsh or higher ground, river-meadow'. ?Baylham, ?Brantham, ?Farnham, ?Hitcham, ?Horham, ?Parham, ?Tangham, Thelnetham, Welnetham.

hangra OE 'wooded slope'. Rishangles.

hār OE 'hoar, grey'. ?Hargrave.

hara OE 'hare'. ?Hargrave.

haven ME 'harbour'. Minsmere Haven.

hēah (dative case **hēan**) OE 'high, chief'. Henham, Henley, Higham (x 2).

h(e)ald OE 'refuge, shelter (for livestock)'. Hawstead.

hecc OE 'hatch-gate'. ?Hitcham.

hecg OE 'hedge'. Hessett, ?Hitcham.

henn OE 'hen (of wild bird)'. Henstead.

hēope OE 'rose-hip'. ?Hepworth.

heorde-wīc OE 'herd farm, farm for livestock'. Hardwick Manor.

heorot OE 'hart, stag'. Hartest.

hey ME (OE **(ge)hæg**) 'enclosure'. Leavenheath.

h(i)elde OE slope'. Icknield Way.

hlāw OE 'tumulus, mound, hill'. Buxlow Manor, Lawshall, Thurlow.

***hlīg** OE 'shelter, refuge'. Layham.

hlid-geat OE 'swing-gate'. Lidgate.

hlyn OE 'maple-tree'. ?Linstead.

hōh OE 'heel of land, projecting hill-spur'. Culpho, Dallinghoo, Hoo Green, Iken, Sutton Hoo, Wixoe.

hōh-sinu OE 'heel sinew, hock-shaped spur of land'. Hoxne.

hol OE 'a hole or hollow'. Holbrook, Hollesley, ?Holton, ?Holton St Mary.

holt OE 'wood, thicket'. Bergholt, Occold, Ramsholt, Southolt.

hop OE 'piece of enclosed land in marsh, small enclosed valley'. Hopton (x 2).

***horning** OE 'horn-shaped feature, bend'. Horringer/Horningsheath.

horu OE 'filth, dirt, mud'. Horham.

hramsa OE 'wild garlic'. Ramsholt.

hratele OE 'rattle' (plant-name). ?Rattlesden.

hrēod OE 'reed, rush, reed-bed'. ?Rede, ?Redgrave.

hring OE 'ring, circular feature'. ?Ringsfield, ?Ringshall.

hrīs OE 'brushwood'. Rishangles.

hrís OScand. 'brushwood'. Risby.

***hruna** OE 'tree-trunk'. ?Rumburgh.

hulver ModE dialect (ME **hulvere**) 'holly'. Hulver Street.

hundred OE 'administrative division of the county, probably originally consisting of 100 hides'. Hundred River (x 2).

***huntere** OE 'hunter'. Hunston.

hūs OE 'house'. Bower House Tye, Onehouse.

hwæte OE 'wheat'. Whatfield.

hwearf OE 'wharf, shore'. Wherstead.

hwēol OE 'waterwheel or other circular feature'. ?Welnetham.

*(h)wifer OE 'unstable, shaking'. ?Withermarsh.

*hwip(p)e OE 'brushwood'. Whepstead.

hyll OE 'hill'. Beacon Hill, Haverhill.

*hylte OE 'wood'. Icknield Way.

*hyrning OE 'horn-shaped, curving hill'. Herringswell.

hyrst OE 'wooded hill'. Hartest.

hysse OE 'tendril-like plant'. ?Hussey Green.

hȳth OE 'landing-place or harbour, inland port'. Covehithe, Lakenheath.

inferior Latin 'lower, nether'. Rickinghall Inferior.

-ing OE suffix 'place or stream characterized by, place belonging to'. ?Cowlinge, ?Milden, Nedging, ?Tattingstone, Wratting.

-ing- OE connective particle implying 'associated with, called after'. ?Assington, Kedington, ?Offton, ?Pannington, Tannington, Troston, Whitton, ?Worlington.

-inga- OE genitive (possessive) case of **-ingas**. Aldringham, Badingham, Benningham, Barningham, Bedingfield, Cretingham, Dallinghoo, Dunningworth, Finningham, Framlingham, Fressingfield, Gislingham, Helmingham, Herringfleet, Heveningham, Honington, Huntingfield, Icklingham, Kessingland, Lakenheath, Letheringham, *Luthinglond* (*see* Lake Lothing), Mettingham, Monewden, Poslingford, Redlingfield, Rickinghall, Waldingfield, Waldringfield, Wetheringsett, Whittingham, Willingham, Wingfield, Worlingham, Worlington, Worlingworth.

-ingas OE plural suffix 'people of, family or followers of, dwellers at'. Barking, Great & Little Bealings, Chickering, ?Cowlinge, Creeting, Exning, Gedding, Gipping, Glevering, ?Milden, Shimpling, Swefling.

karl OScand. 'freeman, peasant'. Carlton, Carlton Colville.

kirkja OScand. 'church'. Kirkley, Kirton.

konungr, kunung OScand. 'king'. Coney Weston.

lacu OE 'small stream, side channel'. ?Lakenheath.

læfer OE 'rush, reed, iris'. ?Livermere.

læs OE 'pasture, meadow-land'. Beccles.

lake ModE dialect (OE *lacu*) 'water-course', ModE **lake** (ME *lake*) 'pool'. Lake Lothing.

land OE 'tract of land, estate, cultivated land'. Breckland, Kessingland, *Luthinglond* (*see* Lake Lothing), The Sandlings, Shelland, Swilland.

lang OE 'long'. Landguard, Langham, Langton Green.

lēac OE 'leek, garlic'. Lackford.

lēah OE 'wood, woodland clearing or glade'. Badley, Bentley, Bixley, Bradley, Brockley (x 2), Butley, Cookley, Cranley, Eleigh (Brent & Monks), Fordley,

Gazeley, Hadleigh, Haughley, Hemley, Henley, Hinderclay, Hollesley, Kirkley, Martley Hall, Oakley, Otley, Shelley, Shotley, Sotterley, Trimley, Westley, Yaxley.

līeg, lēg OE 'fire, beacon'. Leiston.

lifer OE 'liver'. ?Livermere.

līn OE 'flax'. ?Linstead.

little ModE. Little Green, Little London, Little Ouse.

lundr OScand. 'small wood or grove'. Lound.

mǣd OE 'meadow'. Metfield, Shipmeadow.

mǣl OE 'cross, crucifix'. ?Melton.

magna Latin 'great'. Fakenham Magna, Linstead Magna, Thornham Magna, also in early forms of names like Great Barton, Great Bealings, etc.

market ME (from OFr) 'market'. Market Weston, Needham Market, Newmarket, Stowmarket, Wickham Market.

maypole ModE. Maypole Green (x 2).

mearth OE 'marten'. Martley Hall.

melde OE 'orach'. ?Milden.

mere OE 'pond, pool, lake'. Bosmere, Livermere, Minsmere, Rushmere (x 2), Semer, Sicklesmere.

mersc OE 'marsh'. Withermarsh.

micel, mycel OE 'great, large'. Mickfield.

middel OE 'middle'. Middleton.

monachus Latin (genitive plural *-orum*) 'monk'. Monks Eleigh.

mon(e)ke ME (**munuc** OE) 'monk'. Monks Eleigh, Monk Soham.

mōt OE 'moot, meeting, assembly'. ?Mutford.

mūla OE 'mule'. ?Moulton.

myln OE 'mill'. Barton Mills, Long Melford, Mellis, Mells, ?Melton, Mill River, Pin Mill.

næss OE, **ness** ME 'promontory, headland'. Orford Ness, Thorpeness.

nēd OE 'need, poverty'. Needham Market, Needham Street.

netel(e) OE 'nettle'. Nettlestead.

níu OScand. 'nine'. ?Newbourne.

nīwe, nēowe OE 'new'. ?Newbourne, Newmarket, Newton (x 3), Nowton.

north OE 'north'. *Northales* (*see* Covehithe), North Cove, Norton.

ōra OE 'shore, flat-topped ridge'. Orford.

pāl OE 'pole, stake'. Palgrave.

parva Latin 'little'. Linstead Parva, Thornham Parva, and in early forms of names like Little Bealings, Little Blakenham, etc.

peddere ME 'pedlar'. Peddars Way.

peru OE 'pear(tree)'. Parham.

pinn OE 'wooden pin, peg'. Pin Mill.

***pisen** OE 'growing with peas'. Peasenhall.

plega OE 'play, games, sport'. Playford.

pōl OE 'pool, pond'. Polstead, Walpole.

prēost OE 'priest'. Preston St Mary.

rēad OE 'red'. ?Redgrave.

***rendel** OE 'border, edge or strip of land'. ?Rendlesham.

***rēod** OE 'clearing'. ?Rede.

***rinde** OE 'hill, edge, border'. ?Rendham.

rotten ModE 'soft, boggy (of soil)'. Rotten End.

rowe ME 'row of houses, hamlet'. Beck Row, Holwell Row, West Row.

rūh OE 'rough', also as noun 'rough ground'. Rougham Green.

rūm OE 'wide'. ?Rumburgh.

rygen OE 'growing with rye'. Raydon, Reydon.

rȳmed OE 'cleared'. ?Rendham.

***rysc** OE 'rush'. Rushbrooke, Rushmere (x 2).

***sā** OE 'lake, pool'. Soham (Earl & Monk).

sǣ OE 'lake, pool'. Semer.

sǣte OE 'dwellers, settlers'. Elmsett.

sand OE 'sand'. St Cross South Elmham, The Sandlings.

scēad OE 'boundary'. Shadingfield.

scēap OE 'sheep'. Shipmeadow.

scelf OE 'shelf of level (or gently sloping) ground'. Shelland, Shelley.

***scēot** OE 'steep slope'. ?Shotley.

Seaxe OE 'Saxons'. Saxham.

sele OE 'dwelling, house, hall'. ?Lawshall.

***(ge)sell** OE 'shelter (for animals)'. ?Lawshall, ?Ringshall, Stradishall.

(ge)set OE 'dwelling, stable, fold'. Great Bricett, Forncett, Hessett, Wetheringsett, Wissett.

shingle ModE 'pebbles'. Shingle Street.

sīcel OE 'small stream'. Sicklesmere.

skeith OScand. 'race-course (for horses)'. Wickham Skeith.

***snæp** OE, **snap** OScand. 'poor boggy pasture'. Snape.

***speoht** OE 'green woodpecker'. Spexhall.

***stæfer** OE 'stake, post'. Staverton.

stān OE 'stone, standing stone, boundary stone'. Chediston, Stanningfield, ?Stansfield, Stanstead, Stanton, Stonham.

*stānen OE 'stony'. Stanningfield.

stede OE 'enclosed pasture, place, site'. Belstead, Boxted, Harkstead, Hawstead, Henstead, Instead, Linstead, Nettlestead, Polstead, Saxtead, Stanstead, Whepstead, Wherstead.

stoc OE 'outlying farmstead or hamlet, secondary or dependent settlement'. Stoke, Stoke Ash, Stoke by Clare, Stoke-by-Nayland, Tostock.

stock ModE 'tree-stump'. Ringshall Stocks.

stofn OE, OScand. 'tree-stump'. Stoven.

stōw OE 'assembly place, holy place'. Felixstowe, Stowlangtoft, Stowmarket, Stowupland, West Stow.

strǣde OE 'pace, stride'. ?Stradbroke.

strǣt OE 'Roman road, paved road'. ?Stradbroke, Stradishall, Stratford St Andrew, Stratford St Mary, Stratton.

street ModE, **strete** ME (from OE *strǣt*) 'street of houses, hamlet'. Ash Street, Brockford Street, Brome Street, Chilton Street, and many other names.

stūt OE 'gnat. ?Stuston.

*stūt OE 'stumpy hillock'. Stutton.

superior Latin 'higher, upper'. Rickinghall Superior.

sūth OE 'south'. South Cove, Southolt, Southwold, Sudbourne, Sudbury, Suffolk, Sutton.

sūtherra OE 'southern'. Sotherton.

swelle OE 'rising ground'. ?Bromeswell.

swīn OE 'swine, pig'. Swilland.

syle, sylu OE 'boggy or miry place'. Syleham.

tang OE 'spit of land'. Tangham.

thel OE 'plank bridge'. ?Thelnetham.

thing-haugr OScand. 'assembly mound'. Thingoe Hill.

thorn OE 'thorn-tree'. Thorington (x 2), Thorndon, Thorney Green, Thornham.

thorp OScand. 'secondary settlement, dependent outlying farmstead or hamlet'. Ashfield cum Thorpe, Blackthorpe, Ixworth Thorpe, Thorpe (x 4), Thorpe Morieux, Thorpeness, Thorp Hall, Westhorpe.

*thride OE 'deliberation'. ?Thurlow.

thrȳth OE 'warrior'. ?Thurlow.

thveit OScand. 'woodland clearing, meadow, paddock'. Thwaite.

thyrne OE 'thorn-tree'. Thorington (x 2).

toft OScand. 'site of a house or building, curtilage, homestead'. Lowestoft.

tōt OE 'look-out place'. Tostock.

trēow OE 'tree'. Pettistree.

tūn OE 'farmstead, estate, manor, village'. Acton, Alderton, Alpheton, Alton, Ampton, Assington, Assington Green, Athelington, Bacton, Barnardiston, Belton, Beyton, Bildeston, Blundeston, Boyton (x 2), Brampton, Brandeston, Browston Green, Carlton, Carlton Colville, Chelmondiston, Chevington, Chilton (x 3), Clopton (x 2), Coney Weston, Corton, Cotton, Dennington, Denston, Drinkstone, Easton (x 2), Edwardstone, Erwarton, Euston, Flempton, Flixton (x 2), Flowton, Freston, Friston, Fritton, Grimston(e), Gunton, Hacheston, Harleston, Hasketon, Hemingstone, Holton, Holton St Mary, Honington, Hopton (x 2), Hunston, Kedington, Kenton, Kettlebaston, Kingston, Kirton, Langton Green, Leiston, Levington, Melton, Middleton, Moulton, Nacton, Naughton, Newton (x 3), Norton, Nowton, Offton, Oulton, Pannington, Peyton, Preston St Mary, Sapiston, Sibton, Somerleyton, Somerton, Sotherton, Sproughton, Stanton, Staverton, Stratton, Stuston, Stutton, Sutton, Tannington, Tattingstone, Theberton, Thorington (x 2), Thrandeston, Thurleston, Thurston, Thurston End, Troston, Ubbeston Green, Ulveston, Walton, Wenhaston, Westleton, Weston (x 2), Whitton, Winston, Wissington, Woolverstone, Wootten Green, Worlington, Wyverstone.

*tūn-stall OE 'site of a farm, farmstead'. Tunstall.

tye ModE dialect (from OE **tēag**) 'large common pasture'. Barking Tye, Battisford Tye, Bower House Tye, Kersey Tye, Lindsey Tye, Nedging Tye, Willisham Tye, and other names in south Suffolk.

ūf OE 'owl'. Ousden.

uplande ME 'higher land or district (in a parish)'. Stowupland.

vestr OScand. 'west, westerly'. Westhorpe.

(ge)wæd OE 'ford, crossing-place'. Cattawade, Wade.

wægn OE 'wagon, cart'. Wangford.

(ge)wæsc OE 'flood'. ?Washbrook.

wæsce OE 'place for washing (sheep or clothes)'. ?Washbrook.

*wagen OE 'quagmire'. Waveney.

wald, weald OE 'woodland, forest'. Southwold, Waldingfield.

walh OE 'Briton, Welshman'. Walpole, Walton.

wang OE 'open ground'. Wangford.

weg OE 'way, track, road'. Icknield Way, Peddars Way, Weybread.

wella OE 'spring, stream'. Badwell Ash, Bardwell, Bradwell, Brightwell, ?Bromeswell, Elmswell, Eriswell, Herringswell, Holwell Row, Kentwell Hall, Orwell, Sizewell, Wordwell, Worlington.

wenn OE 'tumour, hillock'. ?Wenham.

wente ME 'path, track'. Wentford.

west OE 'west, western'. Westhall, Westhorpe, Westley, Weston (x 2), West Row, West Stow.

*wester, westerra OE '(more) westerly'. Westerfield.

wether OE 'wether sheep'. Wetherden, ?Withersdale Street, Withersfield.

wīc OE 'specialized farm', also 'trading settlement, harbour'. Dunwich, Ipswich, Walberswick, Wyken Hall.

wīc-hām OE 'homestead associated with an earlier Romano-British settlement'. Wickhambrook, Wickham Market, Wickham Skeith.

wīg OE 'heathen shrine or temple'. ?Wingfield.

*wilig OE 'willow-tree'. Walsham le Willows, Wilby, Wilford.

worth, wyrth OE 'enclosure, enclosed farmstead or settlement'. *Beadriceswyrth* (*see* Bury St Edmunds), Braiseworth, Chelsworth, Dagworth, Dunningworth, Halesworth, Hepworth, Horringer, Ickworth, Ixworth, Poslingford, Timworth, Ufford, Worlingworth, Wortham.

wrætt OE 'crosswort, hellebore'. Wratting.

*wride OE 'winding'. Wordwell, Worlington.

wudu OE 'wood'. Hazelwood, Woodbridge, Wootten Green.

wulf-pytt OE 'pit for trapping wolves'. Woolpit.

*wynn OE 'pasture land'. ?Wenham.

SELECT BIBLIOGRAPHY FOR FURTHER READING

Cameron, K., *English Place-Names*, new edition (London 1996)

Carroll, J. and Parsons, D. N. (eds.), *Perceptions of Place: 21st Century Interpretations of English Place-Name Studies* (Nottingham 2013)

Dymond, D. P. (ed.), *Hodskinson's Map of Suffolk in 1783* (Dereham 2003)

Dymond, D. P. and Martin, E., *An Historical Atlas of Suffolk* revised edition (Ipswich 1999)

Dymond, D. P. and Northeast, P., *A History of Suffolk*, revised edition (Chichester 1995)

Ekwall, E., *The Concise Oxford Dictionary of English Place-Names*, 4th edition (Oxford 1960)

Gelling, M., *Signposts to the Past* (London 1978)

Gelling, M., *Place-Names in the Landscape* (London 1984)

Gelling, M., 'A Chronology for Suffolk Place-Names' in *The Age of Sutton Hoo*, edited M. O. Carver, pp. 53-64 (Woodbridge 1992)

Gelling, M. and Cole, A., *The Landscape of Place-Names* (Stamford 2000)

Hart, C. R., *Early Charters of Eastern England* (Leicester 1966)

Mills, A. D., *A Dictionary of British Place Names*, revised edition (Oxford 2011)

Reaney, P. H., *The Place-Names of Essex*, English Place-Name Society volume 12 (Cambridge 1935)

Reaney, P. H., *The Place-Names of Cambridgeshire and the Isle of Ely*, English Place-Name Society volume 19 (Cambridge 1943)

Rumble, A. (ed.), *Domesday Book: Suffolk* (Chichester 1986)

Sandred, K. I. (and Lindström, B.), *The Place-Names of Norfolk*, English Place-Name Society volumes 61, 72, 79 (Nottingham 1989, 1996, 2002)

Scarfe, N., *Suffolk in the Middle Ages* (Woodbridge 1986)

Scarfe, N., *The Suffolk Landscape*, new edition (Chichester 2002)

Skeat, W. W., *The Place-Names of Suffolk* (Cambridge 1913)

Smith, A. H., *English Place-Name Elements*, English Place-Name Society volumes 25 and 26 (Cambridge 1956)

Watts, V. E., *The Cambridge Dictionary of English Place Names* (Cambridge 2004)